A SUMMER
REMEMBERED
~a memoir~

A SUMMER
REMEMBERED

~*a memoir*~

JOHN E. FLEMING

SILVER MAPLE PUBLICATIONS   •   YELLOW SPRINGS, OHIO

Printed in the United States of America

The Text of this book is composed in
Georgia

Cover Art Design by
Tod Tyslan

Cover Photograph courtesy of
Norman Duckworth

Book Design and Composition by
Tod Tyslan

Fleming, John
A summer remembered / John Fleming.
p. cm.
LCCN 2005900740
ISBN 0-9708970-2-2

1. Fleming, John 2. Historians—United States
—Biography. 3. African American Historians—United
States—Biography. 4. African Americans—North Carolina
—Morganton—History—20th century. 5. Morganton (N. C.)
—History—20th century.   I. Title.

E175.5.F5486A3 2005   973'.0496073'0092
QBI05-800209

Published by
Silver Maple Publications
Yellow Springs, Ohio

Dedicated, with love, to my family

A SUMMER
REMEMBERED

~a memoir~

C O N T E N T S

PROLOGUE

Fifty years have come and gone since the summer of 1956; but I remember the summer I turned twelve years old as if it were yesterday. Like a birthmark that stays on the skin throughout our lives adjusting itself to our weight and height, the summer of 1956 placed an indelible mark on my life that remains with me to this day. That summer focused and defined my youth in a way that I have never forgotten. The summer of 1956 became the prism through which I finally began to learn who I was as a young African-American man. It was also the summer that taught me the real meaning of family and community and the importance of being deeply anchored in both.

My community in Morganton, North Carolina, was especially rich in the values and aspirations that have traditionally sustained and nurtured African-American communities throughout the south, where we survived and flourished despite the serious and often violent obstacles we faced in building strong families and communities. I remember my school, Olive Hill School, a modest one-story red brick building with a basement that housed all twelve grades. According to the School Board in Morganton, the land for Olive Hill School had been purchased from my grandmother, Rebecca

Fleming. However, the information passed down in my family indicated that Big Momma (my paternal grandmother) had donated the land for a colored school.

I remember how important my family was to me when I was growing up in Morganton, especially my maternal grandmother Margaret Henessee (Momma), my paternal grandparents William and Rebecca Fleming (DePapa and Big Momma), My Aunt Lillian, and my parents James and Mary Fleming. I remember how my father worked three jobs when we were small. He got up early every morning and went to work at the Drexel Furniture Factory in town. When he got home from the furniture factory, he would eat an early dinner around four o'clock in the afternoon and leave for his second job making picture frames for Greene's Photography Studio. Daddy also worked a third job driving a cab from 8:00 P.M. to midnight. He worked hard so he could make a good life for his family, which included building a small house next to his father's home for his wife and three children. I remember how hard my mother worked as a full-time dietician at Olive Hill School and as a full-time homemaker taking care of us three children, cooking all the meals, washing all the clothes and taking care of my father and all the other demands placed on her as a mother and wife.

I remember our neighborhood on West Concord Street before the street was paved and nobody in the neighborhood had much grass. My Aunt Lillian would tie the ends of tree branches together so that we could sweep the yard. I remember that my favorite pattern was the African knot and how pretty it looked when I finished sweeping the yard. I remember working in our backyard garden with my Aunt Lillian and my paternal grandfather DePapa and the security and satisfaction I got from just being around them as they went about their daily activities. They always managed to make a place for me and the other grandchildren when we showed up to help. We grandchildren were never a nuisance. We were family; and the patience and love they showed us, even when we were being naughty rather than helpful, clarified the value of being deeply rooted in family and the meaning of family ties in a way that remains with me to this day.

I remember my father's older brother, Elliard, even though he died before I was born. Elliard was DePapa and Big Momma's first child to go off to college. Aunt Lillian often talked about how smart he was and how proud the family had been to send a son off to college because DePapa had been the son and grandson of slaves. Elliard was a student at Johnson C. Smith College in Charlotte, North Carolina; there was no high school for colored in Morganton. He was very bright, one of the best students in his class, and the family had such high hopes for him. Elliard was killed in a random act of racial violence. While he was walking near the campus at Johnson C. Smith, some racists threw some bricks at him. One of the bricks hit him at the base of his brain and killed him instantly. His killer was never found.

I remember my cousin, J.W., my Aunt Emily's son. One summer, when I was five years old, J.W., who was 17, took me with him from Morganton to Jacksonville, North Carolina, on the Trailways bus. We had to sit in the back of the bus where the heat, loud noise and oily smell of the engine made the trip hard on a five year old. That was in 1949. Two years later, J.W. joined the Marines and at 19 years of age, he was shipped off to the Korean War. One Saturday afternoon in July of 1951, our family received word that J.W. had been killed in action in Korea. My Aunt Emily never got over the death of her only child who could not sit in the front of a bus in North Carolina, but had been killed fighting in distant Korea for the freedom that his own country denied him at home.

I remember the spring and summer evenings we spent in DePapa's front yard under the shade trees when the weather was good. While I didn't recognize the feeling at the time, I now realize that those evenings were very secure and comforting times for me sitting there with my elderly relatives enveloping me and the other grandchildren with the living, breathing embodiment of what family truly means. There were usually my grandfather, his brother, his sister, my parents, my aunt, several cousins of my father and us grandchildren. These relatives were the literal roots of my family while they lived, giving us the advantage of their knowledge, wisdom, humor and love simply by spending a cool, relaxing evening under the shade trees in the front yard of DePapa's house.

I remember the important role Slades Chapel African Methodist Episcopal (AME) Zion church played in my father's family. My paternal great grandfather, Isaac, and his father, Alfred, were founding members of Slades Chapel AME, which was established in 1881. However, Slades Chapel grew out of an even older African-American church, Gaston Chapel AME, which was founded in 1868. These churches were the heart and soul of a significant segment of the African-American community in Morganton and provided spiritual comfort and material support for their members. Children joined the church, attended Sunday school, church services, Bible classes, and vacation Bible school. They joined the choir, the usher board and the missionary society. They became elders and deacons. They married in the church, aided the sick and elderly, lived their lives as members of the church and were buried in the church.

I remember the story of "The Old African." I heard this story so often, even as a young child, that I could repeat it verbatim; yet I never tired of hearing my grandfather DePapa repeat it. DePapa said the story was part of our family history and that it taught us who we were. He said that the first African ancestor brought to America on my father's side of the family was named "Tamishan." According to family history, Tamishan was of noble birth. He was said to be a very proud man who could read and write from the Koran and could speak seven different African languages and English. Tasmishan's slave master, Waightstill Avery, was said to be impressed by Tamishan and was also said to listen to him read from the Koran.

However, Tamishan never accepted his bondage and was eventually branded as a troublemaker. Although Tamishan started our family line in America with his slave wife (he left a son, Big Alf, who was DePapa's great grandfather), he hated bondage and was determined to be a free man again in his native Africa. So, he convinced his master, Waightstill Avery, to let him return to Africa in exchange for four slaves who would take his place on the plantation in Burke County, North Carolina. My grandfather, DePapa, thought it worth remembering that an African slave had the power of reason and persuasion to convince his master to give him his freedom under those conditions; and Waightstill Avery did agree to Tamishan's terms. Extant records in North Carolina confirm the deal made between the slave master and his slave, after which Tamishan left on a ship for Africa out of the port of Charleston, South Carolina. However, once Tamishan reached his home in Africa, he couldn't bear to send other Africans into slavery in America. Instead, he paid the ship's captain the equivalent in gold of four slaves to satisfy his bargain with Waightstill Avery. The captain accepted the gold, and Tamishan remained in Africa.

DePapa made certain that all his children and grandchildren learned the story of "The Old African Tamishan." That's why I especially remember my grandfather DePapa, who was a living, breathing reminder to us grand-children that no one can be enslaved so long as they know who they are and where they came from. Tamishan never lost sight of who he was and was determined to return to Africa where he came from. Even as a young man, I often thought about all the stories my grandfather told me about our family, about what proud men his father, grandfather and great grandfather were; about how slavery had not diminished their self-esteem and their sense of themselves as men. They knew who they were and were proud to be men of African descent. I realize now how lucky I was to have DePapa as my grandfather. DePapa was a short handsome man, very dark in complexion with snow-white hair and a long white mustache. He, along with my father, was my role model for what it meant to be a man. I shall be ever grateful to my family and community for providing me with such a rich heritage that continues to serve as the foundation for who I am today, a half century later.

CHAPTER I:
THE BEGINNING OF SUMMER

Just five days before school was out for the summer! It was already unusually hot for May. Being close to the Appalachian Mountains, Morganton, North Carolina, where I lived, didn't get as hot as where my cousin Ike lived down east in Durham. I could not resist looking out the window at the pine trees slowly swaying in the warm breeze. One more hour to go before the bell would ring! I did not hear Miss McKayhan's soft but firm voice reviewing the English assignment for next week.

"Johnny, do you have any questions?" She asked, because she knew I was not paying attention.

"Ma'am?" I responded.

"I said, do you have any questions?" she asked more exasperated than before.

"No, ma'am."

I pretended to write down the assignment as I continued thinking about the next weekend and wondering what time Ike would get to Morganton. (I tried not to let school interfere with the things that were important.) After all, it had been several years since I'd seen Ike. Ike was my first cousin, the son of my father's older brother, Louis, who we called Uncle Louie. In Ike's immediate family, there were Donald, the oldest cousin, then Isaac (Ike) and Judy. Donald was the same age as my older brother Jimmy, and Judy was a little younger than my younger sister Patricia. But Ike and I were the same age, except that he was already twelve and I wouldn't be twelve until August 3, 1956. While Ike and I were in the same school grade, he was six months older than me.

We both would be in the sixth grade the following fall. Ike would be in a junior high school because he lived in Durham, where the sixth grade was part of junior high school. But in the small town of Morganton there was no junior high school for colored students. The sixth grade was part of the elementary school. I would have to stay in "elementary school" until I passed to the ninth grade. I just knew Ike would think that he was more grown up than I was because he was in junior high, but I would keep telling him that we were really still in the same grade.

Olive Hill School was the only colored school in Morganton. According to the School Board, the land for Olive Hill had been purchased from my grandmother, Rebecca Fleming. However, my Aunt Lillian told me that Big Momma had donated the land especially for a colored school. She claimed that colored people seldom got a fair price for land or anything else they sold to white people, so even if the land had been purchased by the School Board, she was sure that the price was so low that Big Momma might as well have donated it. Aunt Lillian also said that there had been several other private and public schools for colored children in or near Morganton before Olive Hill was completed in the 1920s.

Olive Hill was a modest red brick building with a basement that housed all twelve grades. Initially there were only eleven grades. Then a twelfth grade was added and finally a separate high school with the same name was constructed on adjoining property west of the old school. When the old school was renovated, the wooden floors were not removed, so they still required daily oiling. Mr. Ben was the janitor for both buildings. Keeping both schools clean was a lot of work for one man. Sometimes Jimmy and I would help Mr. Ben spread the oily sawdust on the floors that had collected the day's accumulation of dust and dirt. The routine was simple. We would start from the back of the classroom and throw sawdust evenly across the floor and then push the sawdust over the floor toward the front of the room, moving each row of desks as we proceeded. The oil-infused sawdust left a pleasantly clean smell to each room and masked the accumulated smell of 30 sweating school children at the end of a hot day in May.

The Hollow

My class, the fifth grade, was located on the south, or backside, of the school. In the first, third, fourth and fifth grade classrooms, the windows faced the playground, the colored cemetery in the distance, and South Mountain on the even more distant horizon. To the left of the playground, facing south, were the woods that extended far beyond the school and cemetery to the train tracks south of town. This was our "adventure land." The trees in the woods were tall and straight, intertwined with long, strong vines. Similar stands of trees, sheltering thick underbrush, lined the hillside that sloped steeply from the woods down to the crooked little creek where we loved to play. Over the years, the meandering creek had created a "hollow," extending from the western end of Concord Street where we lived to the train tracks that marked the southern boundary of our adventure land.

At the far end of the hollow was a small dark shuttered house, which was our self-imposed northern boundary. Peg Leg Jim lived in the house alone. While none of us kids ever saw Old Jim, we were all afraid to go by the hollow at night for fear of seeing him. People in the neighborhood said that Old Jim would grab bad children by the neck and drag them to his house, and they would never be seen again. While none of us ever actually knew of anyone who had suffered such a dreadful fate, we just knew it was true. Adults did not lie. Now, Jim only went after bad kids, but we never knew if we had been "good" enough to get by Old Jim without being dragged off, so we were always careful as we passed the hollow.

If I happened to make the mistake of staying at my grandmother's house after dark, I would have to walk home alone at night. Since my grandmother lived at the top of the hill on Concord Street near the northern end of the hollow, I was particularly scared of all the evil things that might lurk in the hollow at night as I walked home. As I walked the distance from her house to my house, I would approach the hollow with caution and trepidation if darkness had caught me out by myself. As I neared the deepest part of the hollow, I would take a quick glance around to see if anyone or anything was ready to grab me. Seeing nothing, I would run for dear life until I reached Miss Frankie's house. It was never safe at Miss Mae Lee's house, because her house bordered the hollow. No, it was not safe until I reached Miss Frankie's house and only then could I stop running and maybe even look back to see if someone or something was following me. Somehow, I felt it was best to know and to see what was out there to get you, but only from a safe distance. In my mind, there was nothing worse than being surprised by a ghost. Yes, it was best to be able to anticipate these things.

I was certainly glad that I had not been in my cousin David's shoes when he "saw" a ghost in the hollow last summer. David had made the mistake of staying over at our house well past dark. He had gone home by himself. The next day he told me that he had heard these moaning sounds coming out of the hollow as he was walking by. Now David was not scared of most things, but he told me that when he heard a voice cry for help, he ran home as fast as he could. While he never actually saw the ghost, in my book, hearing one was just as good as seeing one.

We never made the connection between David's "ghost" and the fact that old Mr. Clark had fallen in the hollow the night before and could not get out. Poor Mr. Clark always drank a little too much. He would weave from side to side as he tried to navigate his way home. I suppose the night David heard "the ghost," Mr. Clark weaved a little too much, lost his balance and fell down the steep slope of the hollow. Miss Mae Lee, who was the self-appointed "hollow patrol," saw Mr. Clark climb out of the hollow the next day. After Miss Mae Lee's husband died, she devoted more and more of her time to monitoring "hollow activities." I guessed that Mr. Clark was none the worse for having slept all night in the hollow.

The incident with Mr. Clark did little to shake our firm belief that the hollow was haunted, however. Consequently, we had to be constantly vigilant because we never knew when we might meet a real ghost; and ghosts were real! Everybody talked about ghosts and spooks. There were certain people in the neighborhood who were more inclined to see ghosts than others. As much as people loved their relatives while they were living, nobody wanted their dead relatives to come back for a visit. If someone mentioned the name of a dead person, someone would always say, "May he [or she] rest in peace." We knew that Peg Leg Jim was not a ghost, but he was some kind of a monster left to our imaginations to define. This made him even more real and frightening. Every story we heard, whether true or false, added fuel to the fire of our imaginations.

Billy Tate, my brother's sometimes friend, lived near the hollow and claimed that he had seen Jim through his bedroom window. We found it hard to believe anything that Billy Tate said. One day we reluctantly listened to Billy's description of his encounter with Old Jim, believing and disbelieving at the same time what he told us. According to Billy, Jim was "...an old wrinkled man with white whiskers and long wild gray hair" that covered his head to the point where you could not tell where his hair ended and his beard began. Billy said, "Man, I tell you, when Old Jim grinned, I saw only two teeth!"

Jimmy was the first to say, "I bet you just made that up! I bet you never even saw Old Jim!"

"Did too!"

"Then what did you do after you saw him?" I asked.

"I didn't do anything. He was only at my window long enough for me to see his face," Billy exclaimed. Even with such a passionate description, we really didn't believe that Billy Tate had actually seen Old Jim, but just to be on the safe side, we never explored the hollow north of Concord Street, or at least not at night and definitely not alone!

Billy was a big boy with a stomach that bounced when he ran. Sometimes when we saw Billy, my brother Jimmy would tell us to run and hide. Since we were the only kids Billy's age, he would run after us, but he was too fat to catch us. Billy wasn't a bully, so I didn't know why Jimmy told us to run. Maybe Jimmy saw Billy as a challenge to his leadership of the group because none of us ever dared to challenge Jimmy.

Going west on Concord Street toward Olive Hill School and my house, the hollow extended from Miss Mae Lee's house to the cliff just above the train tracks. Miss Mae Lee didn't like for us to play in the hollow near her house. She would yell, "You children stop playing down there before you make my house cave in!" But Jimmy told us that our playing in the hollow could not possibly cause her house to cave in, so we continued to play.

Miss Mae Lee's house was situated kind of funny anyway. Her yard rose so steeply from the hollow, that the back of the house required a twelve-foot foundation to bring it level with the street. Miss Mae Lee was a strange woman. After her husband died, everything made her nervous. Except for the Tates, she lived the closest to Peg Leg Jim. I never heard her say a bad word about Old Jim and his odd behavior. She must not have been afraid of him living so close.

Yet neither Miss Mae Lee nor any one else could keep us out of the hollow. The hollow was its own living, breathing environment. The creek that divided the hollow's steep hills was full of crawdads, minnows, and tadpoles. There were snakes, frogs, birds, owls, rabbits, deer, raccoons, squirrels, and spooks. Of course we saw, caught, or killed everything but the spooks, though to me, they were no less real than the rabbits.

We had great adventures in the hollow. We loved damming the creek to make a small swimming hole. We would collect rocks of assorted sizes and start laying them across the stream. Like beavers, we gathered dead tree limbs and small saplings for the dam. We piled wood and rocks repeatedly until we had a mound several feet high. Slowly the water would fill the dam, creating our own man-made lake. Naturally, the vines hanging from the trees were perfect for swinging across the freshly made pond! We never got the dam large enough to create a pond any deeper than about two feet, but still, it was deep enough to break a fall if we slipped from our swing. The water, always as cold as it was crystal clear, flowed effortlessly across the moss-encrusted rocks. We really had to be careful not to fall when walking on the slippery surface.

The "bear cave" was located at the southern end of the hollow, almost at the top of the red clay hill. While I never actually saw a bear, I was sure bears lived in the cave because Jimmy said they did. I don't know how Jimmy found the cave or even knew that bears lived there, but if Jimmy said it, it was so.

One day Jimmy came to me and David, "I got something I want to show you in the hollow." Naturally, we followed him down the driveway to the back of the school, and up through the cemetery to the top of the hollow. We worked our way through the brush and slippery red clay to the ridge that created an overhang. Jimmy said, "See I told you! There it is! I bet you won't go inside, Johnny!"

Either choice I made, I was going to do something stupid. I was terrified to go into the cave, and I definitely did not want Jimmy to know that I was scared to take on his bet. So, I crawled into the cave to a point where I could still see daylight, and where I was sure that Jimmy could still see me in case a bear grabbed me and dragged me off. We knew that bears liked to grab children because Aunt Lucille said, "Bears come out of the woods to grab and eat up children who tell lies." Aunt Lucille, my mother's older sister, was Catholic and always told the truth.

Ring! Ring! The school bell called me back from my adventures and memories.

I heard Miss McKayhan call my name, "Johnny! Johnny! Whatever are you thinking about? Daydreaming, I am sure. Class is over! Go home and don't forget your homework assignments."

I instinctively grabbed my books and ran to catch up with my classmates. Three o'clock was like the continental divide: on one side was the school day and the boredom of class work, but on the other side was freedom and a wonderfully bright sunny day waiting to be explored. It was too bad that most of the day was "wasted" in school. No wonder my mind wandered.

Kinfolks and Neighbors

While the other kids had to travel across town to get home after school, I had only to walk across the street to be home. Somehow I felt like I was missing something. I would see my classmates travel in groups of threes and fours, talking, laughing, and pulling at each other, and I just knew that I was missing something important, but was unsure of just what it was. My house was next door to DePapa's, my granddaddy, who lived with his only daughter, my Aunt Lillian, and her son Tommy. Often, after school, I walked not to my house but to DePapa's house. The two-story, framed house had grown to nine rooms, but when my grandfather bought it, it had only four rooms. Something of interest was always taking place in DePapa's house because of Aunt Lillian. She had never forgotten what it was like to be a child.

When I walked up the driveway, it was obvious to me that my Daddy needed to put some more gravel or cement down. Although Daddy regularly parked his car in the driveway, he never completely paved it. Each time Daddy worked on a project that had some leftover gravel or cement, he would add the leftovers to the driveway. Consequently, our driveway looked like a masonry patchwork quilt!

That day as I approached the backyard, DePapa and Aunt Lillian were working in the family communal garden. Our garden began about 25 feet from the back of DePapa's house and extended another 50 feet to the end of the yard where a wire fence separated our property from that of our white neighbors. The Carsons' yard lay to the east and another family of white neighbors lived to the west of my house. No one had to ask me to help in the garden. I immediately saw that they were digging holes for tomato plants. DePapa was digging the holes and Aunt Lillian was placing small scoops of manure into each hole. I dropped my canvas bag and notebooks next to the steps and assumed my self-appointed job of putting a quart of water into each hole before the tomato plant was set in. I filled a bucket with water, and using an old rusty sixteen-ounce green bean can, I put exactly a quart of water into each hole.

DePapa was fertilizing the tomatoes with the manure that had been given to him by our neighbor across the street, Mr. Wilford Carson. Various members of the Carson clan had always lived next door to my grandfather's house. My grandmother Rebecca Fleming, whom we called "Big Momma," died when I was 4 years old. My Fleming grandparents had 12 children in all, eight of whom were living in 1956. Four of their sons died before I was born. Of the eight living children, there was only one daughter, Aunt Lillian. My father, James, was the youngest. So, on my father's side of the family, I had one aunt, Lillian, and six uncles: Ernest, George, Louis, William, Joseph, and John. I was named after my Uncle John and my maternal grandfather William Emory Hennessee, hence John Emory Fleming. My mother, Mary, was a Hennessee.

Reverend John Carson, the head of the Carson household, was a minister before retiring, and Miss Lucy, his wife, was a housewife. Their children were college educated. Miss Lucille and Miss Esther were school-teachers while Mr. John Martin Carson, the older brother, was the English teacher at the colored high school. He married Miss Frankie, who was an elementary school principal at Willow Tree School in the country. Mr. Wilford, the younger brother, who lived across the street on the same side of the road as Olive Hill School, never went to college. He married Miss Hester Tate from Bridgewater, a small colored community in the country. She looked like a full-blooded Cherokee Indian. She had long braided black hair and something of a hooknose. She spoke with a gentle Southern drawl. She smiled a lot and we children knew that somehow she and the other Carsons had a special relationship to the Fleming family. We even called Miss Hester,

"Aunt Hessie." Aunt Hessie did not go to college and probably had not finished high school. While her lack of formal education stood out in a college-educated family, Aunt Hessie was my favorite of all the Carsons.

Mr. Wilford's house was situated directly in front of his father's house on West Concord. My granddaddy's house and Reverend Carson's house were built on a hill, the second highest point on Concord Street. Reverend Carson's house overlooked the house of his son, just as our house overlooked Olive Hill School. But we all lived on Concord Street, which stretched from one end of town to the other. On the west side of town were mostly, but not all, colored people, while only whites lived on the east side. You could tell where the colored neighborhoods began because that was where the pavement stopped and the gravel roads began.

The last time I had seen Ike was when the city was extending the pavement to West Concord Street. As I was growing up, few streets in the black community were paved. Most were dusty roads, some dotted with gravel. A gravel road meant that well-to-do colored people lived in the neighborhood. The city did not put gravel on roads in the poorest colored and white neighborhoods.

Work on the completion of the pavement of Concord Street was the biggest thing that happened during that summer of 1952! Big, long, yellow bulldozers with large angled blades plowed up and down the street, cutting into our yards and our neighbors' yards. The city must have taken over ten feet from our front yard for the widening of the street. During one of the sweeps of the bulldozer, the sewer line, which came out of DePapa's house at a sharp angle, was accidentally broken. You could actually see the water rush from the toilet in the house as it passed through the broken amber-colored ceramic pipe on its way into the main sewer line. That's when we discovered that toilet tissue floated like little boats in a stream. Ike came up with the bright idea that each of us should go into the house and have a BM, then flush the toilet and rush out to see our doodoo float down the broken drain pipe. We each took turns. First Ike, then me, and then little Tommy; Patricia refused to participate. She said that little girls did not do such things. Yet in spite of her reluctance to relieve herself, like the rest of us she watched the doodoo sail by. There was not a lot of excitement in Morganton and our doodoo boats sailing by in a broken pipe were our excitement for that summer day.

Aunt Hessie's vegetable garden was located on the side of Mr. Wilford's house. She liked to plant tomatoes, cucumbers, peppers, beans, radishes, and a variety of lettuces that she used to make fresh salads during the summer. Mr. Wilford liked "killed" lettuce and Miss Hester could kill the best lettuce in the neighborhood. She would fry bacon until it was crisp and then at the last minute put vinegar and chopped spring onions into the frying pan. She poured this hot mixture over a bowl of lettuce and that was what "killed" it. It was now ready to eat!

Below the house and garden, Mr. Wilford planted corn, and next to the cornfield was the hog pen. Mr. Wilford always had hogs, hound dogs, one or two goats, and a horse. The dogs had their own individual houses. They were homemade with roofs of metal held in place by large rocks and bricks. Each dog was tied next to its house. Old pots were used for the dogs' food and water dishes. The goats lived outside, but were tied to stakes with a long cord. Every few days the goats were moved to another grazing area. The barn for the horse was located at the very end of the yard and could be seen from the elementary school playground. The horse produced tons of manure, which Mr. Wilford shared with my grandfather...

"Johnny! Johnny! That's enough water!" DePapa exclaimed. "You'll drown the tomatoes with so much water!"

"OK." I had not even noticed that the last hole was full of water.

DePapa continued his advice. "Now go back to the top of the row and push the dirt around each of the tomato plants and pour a little more water on top to make sure that there will be enough moisture to keep them from drying out during the heat of the day."

DePapa and Aunt Lillian taught me everything I knew about gardening. At 11 years of age, I thought we had the largest yard in the world. Our garden stretched for what seemed like several acres, especially when you had to pull weeds or pick beans. A chicken coop had once stood on the spot in the garden where the dirt was rich, black, and full of humus. And the garden dirt was also very rich over a sunken hole at the northeast corner of the garden where the old outdoor toilet used to be. When I was little, I used to think the chicken coop seemed as big as a house. A fence had eventually been built around it so that the chickens could roam around in an enclosed space. I remembered the time before the fence when the chickens had been allowed to roam freely all around the backyard. They never seemed to go anywhere, and they were either always eating or always trying to find something to eat.

It took special skills to collect eggs from the chicken coop. One reason chickens don't make good pets is that they poop everywhere and all the time. So when you were collecting eggs, you had to be extra careful where you walked. There were little mounds of black and gray chicken doodoo every-where. It was a minefield. Sometime you would find a chicken still nestled in a nest. I always hated having to put my hand under a nesting chicken to see if there was an egg in the nest. The chickens didn't like it and neither did I. So generally I would try to run the chicken off the nest before looking for eggs. I used to wonder where these eggs came from, but never had time to wait to see. The chicken coop was hot and smelly in the summer. My job was to get in there, grab the eggs and get out as quickly as possible without being pecked by a chicken or a rooster, getting chicken doo on my shoes, or breaking any of the eggs, (which I had been known to do).

The previous year, a chicken had laid an egg in the garden, trying to establish a nest. Then the chicken must have forgotten about it, because we found it several weeks later. Naturally, as children, our first impulse was to crack the egg. Once done, to our dismay we found inside the egg the beginning of the formation of a little chicken. And it smelled really really bad! After that experience, anything that smelled bad was always compared to the smell of that rotten egg.

So the garden was now the beneficiary of the chicken coop. The chicken manure made that area of the garden very rich. DePapa would plant his radishes, lettuce, and other salad vegetables there. The onions, cabbage, and leafy vegetables had been planted earlier in the spring and were now ready to eat. Mother would tell me to go out to the garden and "Pull an onion!" or "Pick a cabbage!" As the onions matured, we would pull them up and hang them in bunches on the walls in the space under DePapa's house. It wasn't really a cellar; it was more like crawl space with a dirt floor and spiders and hopping bugs everywhere. But even in August, the darkened crawl space stayed cool and dry, so that's where we placed the onions and potatoes. It was into this cavernous space that I would have to hunch my way to retrieve onions and potatoes during the wintertime.

I looked up to see Aunt Lillian beginning to hoe a row for the string beans. I took the hoe from her and said, "Let me make the row for you!" I began the long journey (acres!) to the end of the garden. When I looked up, the row seemed to meander like an old river. My Aunt Lillian never criticized; she gently took the hoe from my hands and straightened the row as DePapa dropped the bean seeds into the ground. I scooped the dirt from the sides and covered the beans in the now straightened row. I loved working in the garden with my aunt and grandfather. I gained a sense of security just being with them. They were not our parents, yet they were authority figures who provided stability and a connection to the past for all the nieces and nephews and grandchildren.

Our garden was directly behind DePapa's house. Everyone in the family at one time or another had lived in DePapa's big white house, now in need of some paint. My grandparents had had 12 children—eleven boys and one girl, eight of whom survived to maturity. My father, the last child to be born, was named James, but everyone called him "Toots." Aunt Lillian, the only girl in the family, always said that he was spoiled, but she was among those who must have spoiled him. When he was four, his brothers liked to swing him around by his feet. His hip joint was dislocated by their play. The repair of his hip was poorly done in the 1920s and resulted in the eventual wearing away of his ball and socket. As a result, Daddy walked with a limp.

The photographs of my father in his 20s suggest that he was a strong, tall, handsome man. The way he cocked his wide brim hat to the side of his head made me think he knew how good looking he was. Daddy worked for Drexel Furniture Company. He got up early every morning at the same time and ate a bowl of oatmeal that Mother prepared. He took two sandwiches of livermush with yellow mustard on white bread to work every day. He ate one at 10:00 in the morning and the other he ate for his lunch. Daddy got off work at 3:30 p.m. and arrived home at four. We ate dinner at 4:30 p.m. so that he could be on time for his second job, making picture frames for Walt Greene's studio. After Daddy got married and started a family, he worked at a third job driving a cab from 8:00 p.m. to midnight. He worked hard and saved his money to build a house next to his father's. We children were afraid of him because he was so stern, but I guess he was not so mean as much as he was tired all the time from working three jobs.

Daddy was very good with his hands and could fix anything. He never taught us much along the line of repair work, though. Since we were required to be his helpers, I guess he thought we were learning by doing. But we did not really do any skilled work. Our typical jobs were to hold the flashlight steady, hold the hammer, get another screwdriver, or hand him some nails. He never talked much while working. He never said, "This is how to hammer a nail," or "You should use a saw like this." Daddy was from the old school. He figured that if you watched how something was done once, you should be able to do it the next time.

I felt that there was nothing more boring that just standing in one spot and holding a hammer until Daddy was ready for it, so my mind tended to wander as a way of self-entertainment. Several years earlier, Daddy had decided to replace a portion of the back porch and I was the designated helper on that hot summer day. Daddy worked without a shirt and the heat made sweat drip down his bare back. As far as I could tell, I was doing a fine job holding the hammer when my nose started to itch. I rubbed it with my left hand to prevent the horrendous sneeze I felt coming on. I frantically switched the hammer and rubbed my nose more vigorously with my right hand, but that sneeze just kept coming. When it finally reached the point where I couldn't hold it in any longer, I turned my head so the spray would miss Daddy's back. But, just as I turned, he moved into the path of the wet sneeze. To my horror, the sneeze propelled a blob of snot which landed in the right in the middle of Daddy's bare back! It may still be there because I had not the courage to remove it and I certainly wasn't going to say that I sneezed snot onto his back! No, I just quickly put that thought right out of my mind as I continued to hold the hammer steady.

Daddy demanded complete and total obedience. This meant no back talking, no eye rolling, no whispering under one's breath. We not only had to do what we were told, but also had to do it immediately. If he said, "Come here," we came right then. "Wait a minute" or "in a minute" were not words in our vocabulary. Curiously, when he wanted us, he never called our names. Instead, he whistled. He also used a whistle to call the dog. Yet somehow, we kids and the dog all learned to distinguish whistles. We never came when he wanted the dog and the dog never came when he wanted us.

Daddy believed that both children and dogs should be well trained. Once he tried to get me to train our little fox terrier. I would hold that poor dog up by its two front legs, trying to get him to walk on his hind legs only. I did this until we both were "dog tired." Then I had the bright idea of placing the dog in the corner and propping his front legs against the right-angled corner walls, but that easier-on-me method did not work, either. After I had spent days trying to train that dog to stand on its hind legs, it was Daddy who gave up.

"You have to know more than the dog to train him," was his comment.

I thought to myself, "Well, of course! That was surely a stupid thing to say." After all, I already knew how to stand on my hind legs. So much for my dog-training career.

Of Daddy's brothers, I knew Ernest, George, Louie, Will, Joe, and John. By the time I was half way through elementary school, they were all old and most no longer lived in Morganton. Uncle Ernest was the oldest. I knew the least about him. For a while he had lived in Durham, and then in Virginia Beach. He had married several times. Cousins Josephine and Ernest, Jr., were children from his second marriage. Ernest's first wife lived in Detroit with their daughter Christine.

Uncle George was smart. He worked on the Ohio Turnpike and lived in Oberlin, Ohio. George married a light-skinned lady by the name of Rita, whose family lived in Luray, Virginia. Their daughter, Leilani, was about ten years older than me. She was light-skinned like her mother, with very long black hair. I always thought that she was very pretty.

Uncle Joe had married a schoolteacher and they had one son named Joe Berry. Joe's wife taught school in Durham, but they also had a home in Philadelphia.

John, Daddy, and Lillian were all born within a few years of each other. If Aunt Lillian was my favorite aunt, Uncle John was my favorite uncle. In 1944, the year I was born, Uncle John was a soldier in World War II. He used to tell the story about the time he broke his leg in the military when a horse fell on him. I loved to hear his war stories and would always ask him which leg was his "bad leg" and would immediately jump on that leg.

Most of my uncles on my father's side and my aunts on my mother's side eventually left home for better employment opportunities in larger cities either in North Carolina or farther north. While Uncle Joe went to Philadelphia to work in the war industry, Uncle John was off to Rome, Georgia, for his basic training. He was later transferred to Daytona Beach where, for the first time, he actually saw Jackie Robinson play baseball. For many African-Americans, military assignments during World War II often consisted of providing support for white troops. After serving in France, Uncle John said that he had been assigned to Fort Myers, Virginia, where his main task was to care for the white officers' horses. It was during this period that a horse fell on him and broke his leg. He was discharged and returned briefly to Morganton. From the first time I remember seeing Uncle John, it seemed as if he was always hungry or looking for food. He wasn't that tall, but he had a huge appetite.

After my Uncle Elliard died, everybody expected Uncle John to succeed where Elliard could not because he had died so young. John was enrolled at Shaw University in Raleigh before enlisting in the military. He eventually returned to Shaw, where he completed his B.A. degree. While he was there, he met and married Hortense Gilmore, who was working on a degree in elementary education and music. Hortense had a beautiful voice and was often called upon by family members and church members to sing at weddings and funerals. John and his family then traveled to Oberlin, Ohio, where he attended the Oberlin School of Theology and Hortense studied for her master's degree in education. Their only child, Sundar, was born in Oberlin. After Sundar was born, Mother took Patricia to visit John and Hortense and their new baby. Jimmy and I were left with Dad. That would have been okay, except that Dad could not cook. We ate a lot of scrambled eggs that week.

When Uncle John and his family moved back to North Carolina, they settled in Raleigh, where he worked for the State Baptist Convention. We got to see a lot more of him and often spent our summer vacations with him, Hortense, and Sundar. And, they often came to Morganton, where Sundar would stay with us during the summer. Everybody thought John was a fine minister, but I liked him best as a storyteller. His stories had an engrossing rhythm and cadence to them. My favorite story started:

"Once there lived three men who had nothing left to eat but a slice of bologna. The three pondered the question: Since there was not enough for all to eat, who should get the bologna? One said, 'We should sleep and dream to see who should have the bologna.' The next morning, they awoke and the first man said, 'I dreamed I died and went to heaven, so I get to eat the bologna.' The second man said, 'Wait! I dreamed I died and went to heaven and met Saint Peter at the Golden Gate, so I get to eat the bologna.' The third man said, 'I dreamed both of you died and went to heaven and left me lonely, so I got up and ate the bologna.'"

Of all the children of my grandfather, I loved my Aunt Lillian the best.

She was one of the most beautiful persons I have ever known. Once I was surprised to hear her brothers say, "Sister," as they called her, "was Papa's homeliest child." I couldn't have disagreed with them more. She had lovely long black hair and a hairline that grew low on her forehead. Her skin was a combination of deep dark coffee mixed with the richest cream, producing a nut-brown complexion. It was obvious that she had both African and European features. She and Uncle John looked much alike and both resembled their mother, Rebecca. Aunt Lillian had large feet—much larger than her father's, who wore only a size seven shoe. Aunt Lillian's beauty came from who she was as a person. She was the most generous individual I have ever known. She married Thomas Tapp of Durham and had one son, Thomas Edward Tapp, or Tommy, as we called him.

There were lots of grandchildren in the Fleming family, which meant we had a lot of cousins. We had some very old uncles, so that their children actually seemed more like aunts and uncles than cousins. All of Will's three boys, James, Mickey, and Charles, were years older than Jimmy, Patricia and myself. It was Louie's children who were our age and it was his son, my cousin Ike, whom I longed to see for the summer.

My thoughts were again interrupted by DePapa saying, "Come on, Johnny, it's time to go in." He turned to Aunt Lillian. "That boy always seems to be daydreaming, Sister."

"Leave him alone," Lillian said. "He's not hurting anyone."

We put away the hoe, bucket, and shovel; ate dinner; and relaxed by sitting in the front yard of DePapa's house, which bordered Concord Street. We sat under two broadleaf trees intertwined with wisteria vines, one white and the other purple. The flowers always reminded me of grapes because of the way they hung in bunches. Wisteria grew so profusely in the trees that I thought the vines were part of the trees. This was a favorite place for the family to gather at the close of a summer day. I opened my pocketknife and decided to carve something from the piece of wood I had found earlier in the garden.

DePapa, Aunt Lillian, Mother and Daddy would sit and talk. Sometimes cousin Edie would come over with her mother, Clara Holloway. Aunt Clara was DePapa's only sister. She was a short, dark, frail woman with white hair. Edie was a schoolteacher, but we did not have to call her "Miss Holloway" because she was our cousin.

My great-uncle Noah, DePapa's brother, lived several blocks away. Uncle Noah worked for the Morganton Furniture Factory. He had been the first Negro ever hired at the factory. The Factory day shift ended at 3:30 p.m. By cutting across the back of the schoolyard, Uncle Noah could be at DePapa's house at 3:40 p.m. During the summer, Uncle Noah would have Dixie Cup ice cream for us. This was a real treat! Uncle Noah married Miss Celi. She was very high strung, excitable, and above all, frugal. No one on our side of the family called her "Aunt Celi." It was always "Miss Celi." They had three daughters, Elizabeth, Helen, and Edith Mae, and one son, Oliver. Uncle Noah and Miss Celi's children were all college educated. The girls had become teachers and Oliver a school principal. Elizabeth was the oldest and smartest and was the dominant one of the three sisters. She lived in New Jersey with her husband, Father Eugene Avery, an Episcopal priest. Helen and Edith Mae still lived at home with Uncle Noah and often came to sit with DePapa under the two trees in the front yard.

Before Concord Street was paved, nobody in the neighborhood had much grass. We swept the sand-like dirt around DePapa's house with homemade brooms. Aunt Lillian would tie the ends of branches tightly together to create a yard broom. It seemed important to her and other members of the family that we maintain a neat yard, especially on Sunday.

So, Jimmy, Patricia and I would help Aunt Lillian sweep the yard and make elaborate patterns in the dirt with our broom. My favorite pattern was the African knot. This involved drawing long parallel lines that would curve back, forming a "U," onto another series of parallel lines, finally forming what looked like an interwoven series of eight or ten parallel lines; boy, didn't the grounds look nice after all this was done!

But after the street was paved, Daddy decided to plant grass both in our yard and in DePapa's yard. Since the county workers had torn up the yard so badly, Daddy had the rest of the yard plowed up, too. We then planted grass seed and put straw over the newly planted yard. It was kind of funny because at first we had this great lawn of beautiful green grass. But slowly, a wide leaf variety of grass began to take over until the whole yard was filled with this wild stand of grass.

Jimmy and I had to cut the grass and if we waited too long, the grass would go to seed, sending out a long narrow stem with a tassel on the end. Our little push mower never would cut through that stem. Daddy didn't believe in modern equipment, no matter what the job. Other people had power mowers. Some even had self-propelled power mowers. We had only a push mower that would never cut the grass very well even the first time. We had to go over the same spot several times and even then it would not cut those seed stems. So, while Jimmy cut the grass, I would have to swing the hand scythe to cut the thousands of stems.

Of course, with the push mower, we could never cut the grass close to the house. After we completed mowing the yard, we would have to use a hand clipper to edge the grass next to the foundation and around the bushes and trees. I hated this aspect of yard work because to get the job done, we either had to bend over until our backs hurt or get down on our knees until they were sore. And on top of all of that, we never got paid. Daddy used to say,

"You get paid every day that you live in this house!" I still thought we should be paid in cash.

In the summer, Jimmy and I would have to get up early to cut the grass while it was still wet from the dew. We always wanted to complete our task before the sun got too hot. But for that night, we sat with DePapa and our relatives over the wild green weed that would be ripe for mowing the next morning.

That evening, I overheard Aunt Lillian tell DePapa that Louie was bringing Ike up the coming weekend. The last time Ike had come to Morganton for the summer, he had gotten into trouble several times. Even the most innocent play would often end with Ike saying or doing something that made someone mad. I think we must have been about eight or nine years old at the time, still young enough to enjoy playing on the swings and the sliding board in the back of Olive Hill School. The "incident" occurred around dusk in late August, when it was still bright enough to be outside and cool enough to want to run and jump. The city had just completed spraying to kill mosquitoes. Not only did we love the smell of the spray, but also in our complete ignorance of the danger, we also enjoyed running behind the trunk pretending we were in a fog. The spray did not last long, so we hurried on across the street to the schoolyard. By this time, several other kids had joined me, Ike, my brother Jimmy, and cousin David.

Tommy Avery from down the street was among the children who came by to play. Tommy must have been a little older than us or at least older than me. As we continued our swinging, Tommy and Ike soon got into an argument. I am not sure why they were arguing, but I guessed it was over Sandra Hicks, the cute little chocolate-skinned girl who lived next door to Tommy. Even as a preteen, Tommy Avery was a nice looking boy. He was the middle child of my mother's first cousin, Jimmy Avery. Jimmy was light skinned with curly brown hair. Tommy had inherited all of his father's good looks including his "good hair." Light skin, curly hair, sharp features were the characteristics that made a Negro good looking. While all of the dark skinned girls liked "yellow" boys, I did not know that Sandra was one of Tommy's girl friends or that she even liked him. Tommy had so many girlfriends it was difficult to tell which one he really liked. I am sure that Ike, being from out of town, did not know that Tommy liked Sandra.

I heard Ike say, "You mother fucker!"

"Who the hell do you think you're calling 'mother fucker?' " Tommy yelled.

"Who the hell do you THINK I'm calling 'mother fucker,' " Ike replied.

"Take it back!"

"Make me!"

With that challenge, Tommy was all over Ike, as they rolled in the red clay of the school yard. Whatever "mother fucker" meant, it must have been really bad because Tommy got very angry. I never did see Tommy give Ike any clear, direct hits to the face, but he must have, judging from the blood gushing from Ike's nose and the droplet of blood beginning to creep down the corner of his now swollen lips. My brother finally pulled the two apart. While I helped Ike toward Aunt Lillian's house, Jimmy, being the leader of our group on this side of West Concord Street, told Tommy to go home. As if obeying a parent, all of the kids left the playground for home. When we got to DePapa's house, Aunt Lillian took one look and brought Ike into the kitchen, where she began to clean his face with cold water and a washrag. Ike sat quietly in the kitchen, which was dimly lit by a crystal clear forty-watt light bulb hanging by an electrical cord from the ceiling.

Aunt Lillian's kitchen had not changed much from the time when Big Momma, who had been bedridden with diabetes for several years before she passed away, was still able to cook and clean. As one entered the kitchen through the back door, there was the homemade wood box right next to the cast-iron stove. The stove had four round "burners" of varying sizes that were removable with an iron handle. Only the left two "burners" were heated directly by the wood fire; the right two "burners" received indirect heat and allowed for cooking at a lower temperature.. The wood was placed in a compartment on the left side of the stove and heated the two burners on top and the oven located in the center of the stove. A good cook always knew when to turn the bread or pie to allow for even cooking and to keep one side from burning. As food got done, pots were rearranged on the stovetop away, from the direct heat source to allow for the food to simmer or just stay warm. There were compartments above the stove that allowed for bread and pies to stay warm and protected food from flies. There was always lard in a Maxwell House coffee can on the stove, ever ready to contribute to fried chicken or seasoning for greens or cornbread. I never knew how long that grease stayed on top of that stove. It was constantly being added to and subtracted from. That can was a grease cornucopia! The only time that I can remember it ever being emptied was when I, being ever so helpful, had poured fish grease in the Maxwell House can. Aunt Lillian had cooked catfish for dinner and asked me to help clean up. All the dishes had been washed and the pans were ready for cleaning. The fish grease had cooled, so the only thing left to do was wash the frying pan. You would have thought that I had taken a life from the reaction I received for pouring fish grease into the Maxwell House grease can!

The cast iron double sink was located beneath the window facing the side of Reverend Carson's house. From that window, you could see the Carsons' garden in the back and beyond that, my Uncle Will's house. The sink sat on a cabinet base that had two doors in front where pots, cleansers, and Red

Devil Lye were kept. Next to the sink was the old oak cabinet where dishes were stored. In this cabinet were special compartments for flour, sugar, and other staples. The flour was kept in a tin bin that was attached underneath the lowest cabinet shelf. The bin had a handle attached for sifting the flour as it came out of the bin. I liked to turn the handle to sift the flour when Aunt Lillian was baking. At the far end of the kitchen was the corner cabinet. It was handmade by DePapa's father and there was not a nail in the wood anywhere, even though the cabinet was made of wood, which was worn and had developed a soft patina to the touch from wear. Aunt Lillian had a deep appreciation for those things associated with family. She said that that cabinet was nearly a hundred years old and one day would be mine. Next to the cabinet was the old icebox. Twice a week the iceman would bring ice in his horse-drawn buckboard. Every family had an ice pick to get a chunk of ice to cool lemonade or just for a drink of cold ice water.

DePapa's kitchen floor was made of rough-hewn wood, covered with linoleum. Over time the wood pattern had become part of the linoleum texture. I never knew what the linoleum actually looked like either—the pattern had long been worn out from the amount of foot traffic in and out of that kitchen. Every once in a while, my sister Patricia and I would take a notion to wash that floor until it was perfectly clean. We would get buckets of water and spread the soapy water all over the floor. We would be sure that it was slippery enough so we could slide from one end of the floor to other. We would slip and fall and did not care if we got our clothes wet and dirty from the murky water on the floor. Finally, Aunt Lillian would call a halt to our fun and tell us to clean up the mess so that she could start dinner.

So, there sat Ike in the middle of this room while Aunt Lillian attempted to get his nose to stop bleeding. As I sat on the back steps, I heard Aunt Lillian tell Ike, "The cut in your lip will heal without stitches. You're lucky this time.

Now take off those dirty clothes and take your bath." Ike, ever repentant, walked through the dining room and down the hall to the bathroom and closed the door. I could hear him running the bathwater in the tub.

As Aunt Lillian rinsed out the bloodstained washrag, I said, "What does 'mother fucker' mean?" She turned to stare at me and said, "Those are bad words. You should never use those words! They're ugly and people get angry when called that name." I now knew the consequences of calling someone "mother fucker," but I still did not know what it meant.

So I said, "Is that why Tommy Avery started the fight with Ike?"

"Probably."

Later, I asked Ike why he used such words and why he liked to fight. He quietly said that he did not know.

My House

Still thinking about Ike and fighting as we sat in the front yard under the tree, I heard Mother call from the front of the house with the screen door ajar, "Jimmy! Johnny! Patricia! Come on in! It's time to get ready for bed." (We were always summoned in birth order.) I gathered my pocketknife and started toward the house after saying "good night" to Aunt Lillian and DePapa. Aunt Lillian's son Tommy had already gone to bed. As I put my pocketknife away, I realized that I had not actually carved anything while I was daydreaming about Ike's last visit. I walked down to our house while Daddy remained in the yard.

Daddy never did housework of any type; that was mother's responsibility. Mother washed, ironed, cleaned, cooked, mended, read to us, and still worked outside of the home. In spite of all this work and having had three children, Mother was still a striking looking woman. Like Daddy, she had been the youngest in her family. She had four brothers and three sisters: Elwood, Royal (Uncle Buck), William, Clifton, Lucille, Emily, and Annie Margaret. I thought Mother was the most beautiful woman in the world even with her straight narrow nose. She was tall, thin with a smooth off-white complexion and straight auburn hair. Mother's hands looked perfect; she wore only clear nail polish. She was a caring mother and was as gentle with us as Daddy was stern.

Mother always had a sense of style. Before any of us were born, she and Daddy had traveled a lot, she in her Mouton coat and Daddy in his double-breasted suit. Mother stopped working outside the home after Jimmy was born. We were all born within a year of each other. Mother did not go back to work until we were all in elementary school. Jimmy was in the third grade, I was in the second, and Patricia was in the first. When we were all in school, Mother started working at Olive Hill School as the dietician. When school was out for the summer, she would often take refresher courses at A & T College in Greensboro, North Carolina. Most of the summer, she spent working at part time jobs or cleaning for rich white families. She was always home, though, in time to fix us lunch.

Bath nights were Saturday night and Wednesday night, for that's when we had hot water. The other nights we washed up with hot water that Mother heated on the stove. Our hot water heater was fueled by kerosene. Daddy had to go into the basement and light the kerosene heater to heat the water. After we all had bathed, he would turn the heater off until the next bathing night. This did not seem strange to us. After all, Aunt Lillian had to heat all the hot water that she used. There were some people in the country around Morganton who did not even have running water, hot or cold. It did not seem odd for Mother to have to heat her water on top of the stove for washing and rinsing the dishes on non-bath nights. So just like she heated the water for washing dirty dishes, she also heated the water we used for washing up.

When we first moved into our house, we had to bathe in a laundry tub in the middle of the kitchen. All the water was heated on the stove, and Patricia, being the youngest and a girl, was washed first, then me, and then Jimmy. One night I peed in the tub water and Mother got mad. I don't why I did it. It just came out. Mother had to pour out the water and then heat some more so that Jimmy could have his bath.

I was always doing little mischievous things, like peeing in the waste-basket next to the toilet in the bathroom. One day when I was 3 years old, I just looked down and saw the basket sitting there. It was as if I heard the basket say, "Hey! How about peeing in me?" I just turned around and peed into the basket. When mother found out and asked me why I did that, I hung my head and said, "Dunno'." (I often used that word to explain mischievous behavior.) I could not very well say that the basket had told me to do it. She would have thought I was crazy. No, it was better to be considered mischievous than crazy.

When Mother and Daddy were first married, they had moved in with DePapa and Big Mamma. By the time I was four, Daddy had built a small house adjacent to his father's house. A large weeping willow and a pear tree separated the two houses. There was also a little two-roomed house that sat in front of our house. Aunt Lillian said that her father had constructed that building for his wife, Rebecca. Big Momma had run a little store there that catered to neighbors and school children.

After Mother and Daddy got married, Mother and Aunt Lillian went to beauty culture school in Greensboro. When they returned, the store was converted into "Lil's Beauty Parlor," where they straightened and curled hair with hot combs and curling irons. Neither of them particularly liked the hairdressing business, so Daddy rented the building to Miss Margie and Miss Teensy, local beauticians. Daddy got eight dollars in rent every week, which must have been a lot of money since he only made $60 a week before taxes. After Concord Street was paved, the city renumbered the houses on the street. Because the beauty parlor sat in front of our house, it received our street address. When Daddy realized what had happened, he went to city hall to see what could be done. When he returned, our street address had become a half. I always hated having a one-half street address. It was bad enough having a little house sit in front of our house! I was sure people thought we lived in that little house.

The house that we grew up in was constructed of cinder blocks and had a partially dug out basement. When we first moved into the house, there were four equal sized rooms: the living room, which had a coal burning stove; the kitchen, where the dining table sat in the middle of the floor; our parents' bedroom, adjacent to the living room; and us kids' bedroom, next to the kitchen. Everyone had to go through our bedroom to get to the bathroom. We had a back porch and a backyard with another pear tree. Since the stove could not heat the bathroom, we had a little kerosene heater in the bathroom for our Saturday and Wednesday night baths.

Each bedroom had a small closet, about three feet wide and a foot and a half deep. Our small closet was never really that full even when all three of us shared one bedroom. There was a chest of drawers in our room and we each had a drawer for socks, underwear, shirts, and shorts. There was an extra drawer for my sister. Jimmy and I shared a double bed; and Patricia had her own bed, even though she had to be in a room with us. There was never a door to our room until Jimmy and I moved out and it became Patricia's private room. Even after a third bedroom was added to the house, we still had to go through Patricia's room to get to the toilet. The difference was that now we had to knock first. Daddy had installed a sliding door to give Patricia some privacy, and we had to knock to get permission to go through her room.

By the time we were in middle school, Daddy had made enough money to add an addition to the house. His brother Louie came up from Durham to help lay the cinder blocks. The new master bedroom was attached to the back of the house. Another door was added to the opposite side of the bathroom, to allow Mother and Daddy to enter and exit the bathroom from their new bedroom. Like the pine paneling in our living room, Daddy had their new bedroom paneled in knotty pine. They had a large walk-in closet and a double set of windows on their west wall. The floors were hardwood and were beautifully stained. They moved their dresser, wardrobe, double bed, and rocking chair into their room.

Jimmy and I inherited our parent's old bedroom, which faced the street and the back of the "little house" that had inadvertently received our house's address. Our room had windows on two walls. But the way the house was laid out, everyone still had to go through a portion of our room, then through Patricia's room, to get to the bathroom. Only Mother and Daddy had any real privacy.

During this move, Patricia got all new furniture—a bed, dresser, and chest of drawers. She had her own closet while Jimmy and I had to share a room and a closet. We got new twin beds, but still had to use the old chest of drawers. At the time, I wasn't sure I was ready for twin beds. I had never slept alone! And even though Jimmy was in the same room, I was still afraid of the dark. I still woke up at night with nightmares about being chased by monsters. Whenever I ran in a dream, I would always fall and the monster would grab me, then I would wake up. But monsters or not, we had the twin beds and I had to make the best of it. The really great thing about all these changes, though, was that we got rid of the old wood burning stove and installed central heat. We no longer needed the kerosene stove to heat the bathroom!

CHAPTER II:
FLATHEAD AND
THE ROTTEN SUMMER

There were just five more days until the last day of school. The Saturday after school ended for the year, Ike was coming to Morganton to stay the whole summer. I could never figure out why during the school year, the weekends always passed quickly and the school days went by so slowly. It seemed like the school week went by in slow motion and the weekends flew by; and when I woke up it was Monday morning all over again. But this week was special. Ike was coming to spend the summer.

When I woke up that Monday morning, the sun was already bright with the promise of another hot spring day. We kept our bedroom windows open during the night and the smell of the carbon plant in Glen Alpine was particularly strong as the wind blew from the west. I knew that we would have to smell that pungent odor all morning because the teacher kept the windows open all day during the spring. My only thought was for this last week of classes to end and for summer vacation to begin.

But, as usual, the last few days of school seemed to take forever. I thought that the week would never end and yet, Friday, the last day of school, finally arrived. Ike would not get to Morganton until sometime on Saturday even though his school was already out for the year. Uncle Louie worked for Liggett and Myers Tobacco Company and had to wait until the weekend to drive his family to Morganton.

It was only 9:16 a.m. on Friday, the last day of school, and we had just started our reading lesson. I thought I might not get to read that day since the teacher started with "Doc" Largent, who sat at the other end of the class. I really did not mind reading. Some of my classmates could not read and it was always so excruciating to have to listen to them try to sound out words. I knew it was painful for them to read aloud.

The poor readers would slowly try to sound out each word, "The A_me_ri_can ex_pe_ ri_ence was a a a..." The teacher would say, "noble." And they would repeat, " a no_ble ex_pe_ri_ence."

The class would hang mutely onto every word, forming the word with their mouths as if that might help the poor readers recognize it better. Having them read, however agonizing, at least used up a quarter of the class period. It was always very important to me to use class time doing something other than classwork, especially classwork that might result in my being embarrassed if I were called upon. I could read, even if I could not tell the difference between an adverb and an adjective. I generally knew what a noun and verb were and could pronounce most words.

It was spelling that was my worst subject of all. The class was always divided democratically for spelling bees, unlike when we played ball and the Captains got to pick the members for their teams. They always chose from the best players down to the worse ones. Most of the time, I was not the last person chosen, especially if we played "mixed" ball. There were always girls who could not hit a ball or who couldn't run. Big girls like Libby Peterson could both hit and run. She was almost always chosen early in the lineup. But spelling was another matter altogether.

During the last spelling bee early in May, the teacher had us call "one" and "two" alternatively. All the "ones" went to one side of the room and all the "twos" to the opposite side. My great desire, my all encompassing wish, was to not sit down on the first round. If I could just make it pass the first round, then it would be OK because I knew that Sadie, Jimmy, Marie, and several more might not make it past round one. I really hated it when I had to sit down on the first round. Brenda, Ella Mae, Steve, and Raymond would be the last ones to remain standing. Somewhere in the middle would be Emmajean, Marguerite, Frances, Troy Lee and, hopefully, me.

The Spelling Bee started with Miss McKayhan asking Ella Mae to spell the first word, "administration." That one was easy for Ella Mae. I thought that I, too, could spell "administration." Raymond, one of the smartest students in class, was asked to spell "document," and of course, he spelled it correctly.

The teacher asked Marie to spell "inspiration."

Marie said, "Inspiration,.....inspiration,.....let's see. Use it in a sentence?" she asked the teacher.

Miss McKayhan said, "Spell this word correctly so that you can provide 'inspiration' for the class."

Marie said, "Inspiration.....I n s p r e r a s i o n.....Inspiration."

Miss McKayhan continued with the Bee, "Marie, you can take your seat now. Brenda, spell 'inspiration.' "

"I n s p i r a t i o n.....inspiration."

Soon it was my turn. While I wanted a word more difficult than one syllable, like "cat," it couldn't have too many syllables, or I would never get it right.

Miss McKayhan said, "Johnny, spell 'memory.' " Well, I knew that one, so I said, "M E M O R Y, memory."

Boy, was I glad that was over and I was still standing! After Miss McKayhan had everyone in the room spell a word, it was my turn again and she came back to me with my second word, "retrieve." "Oh, no!" I thought.

"Uh, Retrieve..... 'r e',"....."so far, so good," I thought; and finally, mustering all my knowledge, I said, "r e t r e i v e."

"Wrong!" the teacher said. "Raymond, how do you spell 'retrieve?' " Raymond replied, "R e t r i e v e....retrieve."

I could see Sheila Hicks, Frances Corpening, and Margaret Morris all give me a sympathetic look before I took my place among the dozen or so other students who were already sitting, but that was OK. I was not the first one to sit down and that was the important thing. "Well," I thought, "no more spelling bees for three months!"

Time must be relative because it always runs slower for young people than it does for adults. There is a definite relationship between time and pleasure—the more enjoyable the experience, the faster the time passes. And the reverse is also true—unpleasant events take forever! So there must be different types of time; otherwise, why would a class hour take two hours to pass while an hour's recess is over in a half hour? These were the burning questions I pondered in school. I also thought about how last summer was the longest summer I could remember. It was just an awful summer in everyway. Everything that happened to me last summer had made me miserable, beginning with the end of school.

The Rock

It was almost a year ago in May of 1955 that school was also coming to an end for the year. Everybody was excited and anxious to learn what was in store for them during the summer of 1955. It was hot that year, too! Since Morganton generally had cool mornings even as late as June, it was not unusual for school kids to wear a sweater or jacket to school in the morning. But by 3:30 p.m. when the last bell rang, it was too warm to wear any extra clothes. So usually we would tie our jackets around our waists to free up our hands for other things.

It was a special day. Rather than walking across the street to go home, I was heading down to the *News Herald's* office to apply for a job selling newspapers. Our principal, Mr. Morris, had received word that the paper wanted to hire several colored paperboys. My cousin David and I decided to try out for the jobs. I was to meet David at his house on the way to town. As I walked across the front of the schoolyard, I suddenly felt this excruciating pain in the back of my head. I wore my hair very short and did not wear caps or hats, so there was nothing to cushion the blow when a large rock struck the back of my head.

I thought, to the extent that the pain allowed any thought at all, "Do not fall down. Do not do anything to call attention to yourself." I bent over, nearly falling to the ground. My eyes watered. I thought, "Whatever you do, don't cry." Maybe no one would notice. Holding my head, I turned to look for my assailant, but I didn't see anyone. There were bloodstains on my hands as I pulled them from behind my head. It was blood that was coming from my head! Never in my life had I felt such pain!

The extreme pain immediately brought with it thoughts of my Uncle Elliard. Would I die just like my uncle? Poor Elliard. He had been killed when he was a student at Johnson C. Smith in Charlotte. Elliard was DePapa's oldest, except for the first born who died at birth. Elliard had been the first to go off to college. Aunt Lillian talked about how smart he was and how proud the family had been to be sending a son to college. After all, DePapa was the son of a slave and here was his firstborn son going to college in 1914, just 50 years after the end of slavery! Yes, my grandparents were proud; all the family was proud because it meant that Elliard would be able help the next one go to college and that one would help the next one until all who wanted advanced schooling could get it.

It was a brick that had killed Elliard and a rock that now threatened my life. A white man had thrown a brick at Elliard and killed him instantly. Just like my Uncle Elliard, someone had also thrown a rock that hit me in the back of my head. I thought, "Will I die like my uncle in the prime of my life?" I knew that it was not a white man who had hit me in the back of my head, though. No, it was one of my colored schoolmates. In the distance I heard someone yell, "Bulls eye, Flathead!" But I did not collapse, pass out, or die. My life was spared of a racial murder. Yet I could not help but think of my poor Uncle Elliard, whom I would never know, cut down in the prime of his life because of a senseless act of racial hatred. My granddaddy never spoke of Elliard, but Aunt Lillian, the family historian, often mentioned his name.

Aunt Lillian said that Elliard was very bright, but since there was no high school in Morganton, DePapa had sent Eilliard to Johnson C. Smith, one of the dozens of schools organized after the Civil War to teach the newly emancipated slaves. Like most of these schools, Johnson C. Smith started off as an elementary school and added grades as the students advanced. Even when Johnson C. Smith became a full-fledged college, it kept the secondary school because so many communities like Morganton did not provide a high school for Negroes.

Elliard had completed his high school years at Johnson C. Smith and entered college as a freshman in 1914. Aunt Lillian said that he had been among the top students in his class. She added that back in those days, you never knew when or where a violent act against Negroes might occur. For Elliard, it had been a random act of racial hatred. While he was walking alone from the school library, some white men driving by had thrown bricks at Elliard. One hit him at the base of his brain and he was killed instantly. No one ever learned who had done it.

So on this sunny May afternoon, I thought of Uncle Elliard as I walked with a throbbing dull pain in the back of my head toward town. I stopped at Momma's, my maternal grandmother's, house to get David. For some reason, I never mentioned the rock-throwing incident to anyone.

Momma

I loved my maternal grandmother, Margaret Woodard Hennessee. We all called her "Momma"— her children, grandchildren and great grand-children. Momma and my grandfather, Willliam Emory Hennessee, had eight children: Elwood, Royal, William, Clifton, Lucille, Emily, Annie Margaret, and Mary, my mother. My maternal grandfather, William Hennessee, died when my mother was four years old. Momma lived with her sister Annie, her son Royal whom we called "Buck," and her grandson David. Sometimes when his second wife would put him out of the house for binge drinking episodes, my Uncle Cliff would also move in with Momma. Momma also had several grandchildren: Lucille's daughter Anne; Emily's son, J.W.; Annie Margaret's son, David; Mary's children, Jimmy, Patricia and myself (Johnny); William's children, William, Jr., Corinne, Mary Margaret, and

Betty Jean; and Clifton's children, Charles and Ford.

Momma lived at the top of Concord Street, just two blocks from where we lived. Momma's house was at the intersection between the colored neighborhood and the white neighborhood. Going east toward town, Concord Street was the dividing line between the two communities. On the north side lived some very rich and prominent families and on the south side were some of the colored descendants and servants of those same families.

With Momma literally looking like a white person but living in the black community, it seemed appropriate that her house would straddle the two communities. Momma, her mother, and her grandmother all said that they were colored. But I could not see it. When you looked at them, it was not apparent that they were colored. There was no physical characteristic that would even suggest to the eye that they had a drop of Negro blood. It was something we just accepted as true because they said it was true. But, Momma was the whitest woman I ever saw. One day, when I was much younger, Momma and I had been walking to town and my hand fell out of her hand. She walked ahead of me and I turned and grabbed the hand of a white woman, thinking that it was Momma's hand.

I was not the only one who perceived Momma as being white. Momma once told me that a train conductor had tried to force her into the train car reserved for white people. Momma's older sister Cora lived in Boston, and Momma and Aunt Annie would take turns visiting Cora over the years to help out after each of her children were born.

While I had never traveled on a train, I was familiar with the train station in Morganton. The east side of the station was reserved for white people. The middle was the ticket office and the west side was "For Colored Only." We all went in on the colored side. People in Morganton knew Momma, so no one questioned that she was colored. Momma said that when the white conductor saw her in the car reserved for colored people, he walked right up to her and said, "Ma'am, you're in the wrong car. The car for whites is behind this one."

Momma had replied, "I'm colored," to which the conductor said, "I know a white woman when I see one! You must move before we can start this train." With great reluctance, Momma moved to the next train car, but had felt uncomfortable until she reached Philadelphia. Pennsylvania was integrated and colored people could sit anywhere.

In addition to her sister Cora, Momma had three brothers and one other sister, Annie. The first time I had seen a picture of all of them, I thought that it was a white family. Interestingly enough, only Momma's brother Edward had married a white woman and passed for white. I never knew my Uncle Ed, but I had heard that he lived in New York. My Mother's sister, Aunt Lucille, told me that a number of years ago, Uncle Ed and his wife had come to Morganton for a visit. They only came that once. His wife had known that he came from a colored family, but it surely didn't matter, for he was as white as she was.

Momma must have been a beautiful woman when she was young. Though she stood less than five feet two inches, she was still a commanding figure. In my estimation, she was always old. After all, anyone older than 20 was old to me! Momma had fine straight brown hair that she kept tied in a ball in the back. She wore gold wire rim glasses. She had very fine features and a beautiful smile. She was considered a good looking lady. She had small white hands and never wore nail polish or makeup. Her dress was very conservative and traditional for the 50s. She always had on an apron unless it was Sunday, and then she would wear a fine black dress or a black and white polka dotted dress with a black coat that had a small fox fur collar. She wore black tie up shoes with small heels. She looked and dressed like a "typical grandmother" in a Norman Rockwell portrait.

Momma did not like to talk about the past, but Aunt Annie did. Aunt Annie liked to talk about her grandfather who, accordingly to her, was a doctor who had come from the Charlotte area. She talked about her maternal grandmother, who was named Mona. Aunt Annie said that Mona never wore shoes, even in the wintertime! She attended the White Presbyterian Church. Aunt Annie loved to talk about her parents, especially her father. Her father was named Durant Woodard. Aunt Annie said that he drove a carriage for the state hospital. I had never known my great grandfather, but I remember my great grandmother, Emily Crisp Woodard. She had been a small frail woman. I was only four years old when she died and my memories are of her being in bed most of the time. My great grandparents had had 12 children, but only six had lived beyond childhood.

I did not stay long that day at Momma's. Aunt Annie had locked David in the closet for some reason. I went over to the closet door to check on my cousin. He was mad and talked about running away. We often talked about running away from home as if we were characters in the Huckleberry Finn novel or from the "Little Rascals."

But that day my head hurt, so I did not stay long at David's. I decided not to go to town to apply for the paper route after all, but to return home. I always thought that the distance between where I lived and where David lived was "sooooo" long. After I left Momma's house I had to pass by Miss Celi and Uncle Noah's house, the dreaded hollow, (though I never feared the hollow during the day—it was only at night that I thought about Peg Leg Jim), then Miss Mae Lee's house, Miss Frankie's house, Miss Mae Scott's house, Miss Maggie's house, and Miss Clark's house. Then toward the top of the next hill was Miss Hester's house, and finally Miss Viola's house, which was across the street from my Aunt Lillian's house. It was funny how we identified all the houses with the wives and not the husbands who lived in them. It was absolutely essential to put "Miss" before all names, no matter the marital status.

At School

The noon bell, that announced lunch and recess, ended my painful memories from the rock incident. That bell was like music to my ears because it was the last day of school. I had actually spent the entire morning daydreaming about the horrors of last summer! I was sure that with Ike coming to visit on Saturday, the summer of 1956 would be much better.

Mother was the dietician for both Olive Hill High School and the Elementary School. The younger children ate first in the small cafeteria in the basement of the elementary portion of the school. The cafeteria was under the restrooms. We all knew that according to the building codes, food service areas should not be located under a restroom, especially where the sewer drainpipes were exposed. But these regulations and other laws were never uniformly applied to the colored community, especially when it was not convenient to do so. The School Board needed a place to put the cafeteria and the only place available after the renovation was under the restrooms. So the city looked the other way and that was that.

At the beginning of the week, the teachers would collect the lunch money. We each had to bring our money to the front of the class and each week I would dutifully, if shamefully, march to the front and announce quietly to Miss McKayhan, "My mother will pay for my lunch." We both knew that since Mother was the dietician, the Fleming children did not have to pay. I still had to go through this ritual to reassure myself that Miss McKayhan would not pull me from the line and ask for my lunch money. I would not have been able to stand being singled out with no money.

Our classroom was the fourth in a row of five first-floor rooms on the south side of the building. The first grade had lunch at 11:15 a.m. It was not until 11:45 a.m. that my class was scheduled to eat. Then at lunchtime, we moved as a group down the hall, and passing the last two classrooms, we turned right, down the steps and into the basement. We formed a line around the wall and slowly worked our way up to the counter where the food was served. It seemed that no matter what was on the menu, there were always some kids who would complain. "What's that?" they would ask rudely, or say "I ain't eatin' this stuff!"

But whether or not we wanted or liked what was being served that day, we each received our portion. A typical meal was macaroni and cheese, fish sticks, cole slaw, Wonder Bread, and a bottle of milk. After getting our lunch trays filled, we dutifully sat down to eat at wooden tables and chairs. Each table would seat ten people, including the teacher, who usually sat at the head of the table.

We would all watch as Miss O'Neill's sixth grade class entered the room. Unlike the rest of the classes, Mrs. O'Neill's students usually behaved perfectly. None of them dared make a comment about the food or much else either. Miss O'Neill sat at the table and expected her class to gather around her, where she could keep a sharp eye on each of them and they could watch her. The slightest move of her little finger meant that the person out of place had better get back in place quickly or face the consequences. Just parting her thin lips was enough to make the entire class stop talking.

Miss O'Neill might have been pretty at one time. Now she wore so much makeup, it was hard to tell whether she was still pretty or not. Her hair was always straightened with waves running from front to back. We were never sure if she had "good" hair, but we knew that she did not have any real eyebrows. She painted them on. They were quite dark and easy to see. If she lifted her left painted eyebrow at one of her students, it was a certain sign, one that guaranteed that that student would receive a severe punishment, usually a whipping with a paddle.

That last day of school, Harry Corpening forgot the rules and was talking too loudly. He got the dreaded raised eyebrow, but he didn't see it the first time. Martha Tate told Harry, "Psst! Look at Miss O'Neill!" She had raised her eyebrow a second time. Harry was immediately seized by raw terror. He must have thought to himself, "Oh no, not the raised painted-on eyebrow! Not me! Ooooh, why me?" We actually saw Harry's small body sink into a state of depression. He never said another word during lunch and scarcely touched his food.

My brother Jimmy, who was in Miss O'Neill's class for three years in a row ,said that she was so mean she caused him to lose interest in school. Jimmy had first entered Miss O'Neill's classroom in the fourth grade, and since I was right behind him in school, everyone expected me to be in her class the following year. But, that year Miss O'Neill moved with her class to the fifth grade, which meant that Jimmy would have her for a second year and then, as it turned out, even a third year. Boy, was I thankful and, I thought, lucky! Every day I was even more thankful as I watched her control her class with an iron hand. In addition to Ike coming that summer, I thought how lucky I was that Miss O'Neill wasn't assigned back to the fifth grade. Next year, I would have Mr. Ferris, the only male teacher in the elementary school.

After lunch we would go to the schoolyard to play. The playground was in back of the elementary school and next to the high school auditorium. The sandy ground was an orangey-red color. A lack of rain would turn the dirt into a fine powder that created little puffs of dirt when you walked over it. Running would raise miniature dust storms! I sat on the side of the field, still suffering from my terrible little league experience from last summer.

The Strikeout

Jimmy and I did everything together. I was proud that he was the undisputed "boss" of the neighborhood. Jimmy was 18 months older than I was, so he made all the important decisions. Late last summer, we, or rather, he decided that we would be on the little league team, coached by Miss Frankie. Miss Frankie was married to John Martin Carson, Rev. Carson's son. All the Carsons' were brown-skinned people, but Miss Frankie had light skin with lots of freckles. She was the principal of Willow Tree Elementary School, up in the country. She was very involved in the community and worked with several youth groups. She was what they called a "race woman." She was always doing something to promote the advancement of the community and our race as a whole. Miss Frankie drove a jeep that was always dirty and full of stuff. On the first day of practice, we walked down the hill to her house in order to ride with her across town to Bushelle Street, where the colored recreational center was located.

It was a hot summer morning. Already the temperature had reached 90 degrees. The short ride in the jeep was refreshing as the warm air rushed across our faces. We helped unload the jeep. Miss Frankie had all the softball equipment that we needed for the team. Neighborhood boys had already gathered and were waiting for the tryouts. One older boy rubbed my head and said, "What do you know, Flathead?" I walked away, ignoring the comment, still not understanding why they had decided to start calling me "flathead." As far as I could see, I had a very normal head.

Morganton, like hundreds of communities throughout the South, was segregated. But segregation did not always mean physical division. White families lived all around us, but we did not intermingle. There were segregation laws that provided for separate schools, hotels, restaurants, cemeteries, barber shops, etc. In our town, what was not prescribed by law was accomplished by custom. For example, there were two recreation centers. One was for whites and one was for coloreds, and we had to pass by the white recreation center to get to ours. We had heard that about two years earlier, the Supreme Court had ordered all schools integrated. Our reaction was that we did not want to go to school with white folks! I believe that we were probably afraid because we did not know what to expect. It seemed natural to us that we would have our own recreational center and "they" would have theirs. We did not know what this "integration" thing would mean. For now, for us in Morganton, it would be the status quo because as late as 1955, nothing had changed.

While it would have been nice to go to the center closer to where we lived, we liked our new colored center that had been built only the previous year. It was a modern one-story building shaped in the form of a reversed "L." The recreation center was located at the edge of the all black community we called Bouchelle. From Bouchelle Street proper, one had to walk down the hill to the flat flood plain created by the Johns River to get to the center. Once you entered the front door of the center, you had to check in, and either buy tickets to the swimming pool if that's what you were going to do, or could purchase items from the snack bar to the left. Then you walked into a large, bright, and airy open space that served as the center's multi-purpose room. We played games there and had socials, and adults often used the space for dinners. The swimming pool with bathhouses for boys on the left and girls on the right was situated behind the center. The ball fields were just north of the Center. There were no tennis courts. I guess the Town Fathers thought that colored people did not play tennis. You know, they may have been right, at that. I did not know of any colored person who played tennis. I certainly could not play. But we did have basketball courts and ball fields.

That hot summer day we all lined up as usual at the edge of the ball field for the tryouts; older boys went to bat first and then the younger ones. I was somewhere in the middle. Jimmy was among the older boys and was a good hitter. I knew that he would make the team because he was good at sports generally. While I was not really good, I did not think that I was bad.

As soon as it was my turn, I walked confidently up to the plate and took my stance. I swung at the first ball that was thrown and I missed. "No problem," I thought, "I will surely hit the next one." But I missed again! When I missed the third ball, I saw that Jimmy had a concerned look on his face, one that would soon change to embarrassment. Lawrence Whiteside was pitching and made every effort to help me hit the ball. He pitched me several more balls, all of which I missed. He slowed down the speed of the balls. Alas, all to no avail. "Boy, is it hot!?" I thought. This was not so much due to the 90 degree heat as to the shame I was beginning to feel at not being able to hit the ball. Lawrence even moved closer to home plate as the balls rolled in slower and slower. I missed and missed. Everybody was looking at me! Someone yelled, "Can't you see the ball, Flathead?"

Great. Now everyone would know me as "Flathead, the boy who couldn't hit a ball." I thought maybe I could not see the ball. "That's it! I'll pretend to be blind!" Yes, that was the answer; I could not hit the ball because I was blind. I was willing to accept temporary blindness rather than be embarrassed at being a poor ball player. In a final desperate attempt to allow me one hit, Lawrence came so close to the home plate that I thought I would strike him with the bat. He literally dropped the ball right in front of me. I concentrated on that ball; held a tight grip on the bat, pulled back, and swung with all my might. Somehow, somewhere, someone or something moved that ball to where my bat was and they engaged. The small crowd roared! I heard people scream, "Flathead hit the ball!"

I didn't care what they said. I was just so glad that I had finally hit the ball and was no longer standing there for everyone to see me make a fool of my self. I tried to move to a section of the field where I would no longer be noticed and wouldn't be the center of attention. I sat quietly under a tree. Jimmy came over and asked why I couldn't hit the ball. I did not answer him or any other big kid who walked over to harass me and tried to rub what they thought was a flathead. That was my first and last little league game. And it wasn't even a game. The team had not been organized; we had no uniforms, nothing. Obviously I was not going to get to be on the team, so I should say that that was my first and last "almost game." There was no game for me.

Later, in school when it would be time to be picked to be on a team, any team—softball, baseball, football, basketball, it didn't matter—my greatest dread was to be picked last. As it turned out, while I may not have been the last one selected, my selection was just above Bobby Peterson, who could not see well even with his thick glasses and definitely could not run fast. Only if someone sprained an ankle or broke a leg or arm, was I able to move up to being next to last. Whenever I played baseball, I would select a position where I thought the batter would not likely hit the ball, thus reducing my chances for missing the ball. When it was my turn at bat, I didn't feel I had to hit a homerun, but I prayed that I would not strikeout. I would try desperately to hit even a foul ball. I needed to just hit the ball. I didn't even care if someone caught it. It was just getting a hit that mattered.

So there I sat during recess thinking about last summer, the little league, and being named "Flathead." I kept thinking, "What a rotten summer." I walked back to class still reminiscing about last summer. I passed by James Pinckney, who was in high school. He said, "What 'cha know, Flathead?"

Cracked Eggs

Once I got back to class, I kept thinking, "What a name! Why was everybody teasing me?" I thought, "Even if my head is flat, that's nothing to joke about." Nobody ever thought that maybe this name-calling hurt my feelings, and I was determined not to show it. I didn't want to give them the satisfaction of knowing that sometimes I was teased so brutally that I just wanted to cry.

On top of all that, it seemed that I couldn't do anything right during the summer of 1955. I was growing, but my voice had not changed. I could not detect any other physical changes, except for waking up some mornings with the stiff pajamas I occasionally had. I hadn't quite figured that one out and did not dare ask. No one ever talked about sex or anything relating to sex. I remember Patricia getting a whipping for having a little Snuffy Smith comic book that she said Jackie Foxx had given to her. I learned later that Patricia had been snooping in our parents' room and had found this little comic book in one of Dad's chest of drawers. It showed Snuffy Smith having sex with a woman who was obviously not his wife. Patricia got a whipping, but I was never sure whether it was for snooping in our parents' bedroom or for taking and reading Dad's little sex comic book. I figured that I would be on the safe side and assume that the whipping was sex-related and that in the future, I would just keep my mouth shut on the subject of sex.

I knew I was a klutz when eggs became a particular problem for me. I remembered that when I was younger, I had had no problems (other than the chickens pecking at me) going to the hen house, collecting eggs, and success-fully maneuvering them into the house. Now that I was older, the eggs just jumped from my hands! On Fridays, Mother shopped at the A & P, but during the middle of the week, she sent us to the neighborhood store for perishable items. I remember one time that Patricia and I were going to the store for several items, including a dozen eggs. Wall's store was only two blocks away. We made our purchase and started across Burkemont Avenue. No sooner had we reached the other side of the street than the eggs just jumped out of my hands. The entire dozen broke. I was gripped by fear. I had no extra money to replace the eggs. Patricia said that she was going to "tell it." Her sing-song voice rang out, "Wait to we get home! I'm going to teelll it, I'm going to teelll it!" But it was not until I had actually broken the second dozen that I was finally prohibited from handling eggs.

We looked forward to Mother's Friday shopping trips to the A&P to see what goodies she would bring home for us. When asked to help put up the groceries, we would search for ice cream, cookies, sodas, and comic books. We used to love for Mother to read the comics to us. Now that we were older, we read them to ourselves. After determining what goodies she had brought, and laying claim to our favorites, we would finally get around to putting away the rest of the groceries. That day, I grabbed the eggs, but the carton must have been defective. The top came loose from the bottom. All twelve eggs fell to the floor. Mother asked, "Why are you so clumsy?" Of course I had no answer. But from then on, I was not permitted to handle eggs, cartons of milk, glass jars, or indeed, anything breakable.

That summer I walked in front of a car at the very same spot where I had dropped the dozen eggs. It was bad luck, that corner of New Street and Burkemont Avenue. A car just appeared out of nowhere as I was crossing the street. I immediately put my hands out in front of me and actually touched the car with my bare hands to keep it from running over me. I must have seen that trick on one of the Superman television shows. Instinctively, I tried to stop the car. I was thankful for the quick reaction of the driver and for his good brakes!

While I could very faintly, in the deep recesses of my mind, hear Miss McKayhan review the reading list for the summer, I continued to reminisce about the horrors of last summer...It was also during the summer of 1955 that I had run into a telephone pole. To this day I cannot figure out where that pole came from. I was on my way to town on our bicycle. Jimmy and I had one bike between us, assembled from several different bicycles. We were very ingenious about putting things together. While Daddy never had the time to help us do things, we always had to help him fix a door, build the little house where he kept his tools, cut the grass or paint the house. These were all the things that he wanted to do or had to do. The things that we wanted to do, we had to figure out for ourselves. There was an old bike in the shed behind Aunt Lillian's house. We got it out and managed to find parts from several other bikes. We put them all together and had our first bike. We painted it all one color, black, which was the only paint we could find. We dearly loved that homemade bicycle.

Late one summer afternoon I rode that bike to town. Just before Belt's Department Store, the sidewalk narrowed to the point where the dirt space between the curb and the sidewalk disappeared. The telephone poles were embedded in the sidewalk. It was at this point that I rode that old bike right into that pole. I simply didn't see it! My groin area hit the middle bar connecting the seat portion of the bike to the handlebars and I was in excruciating pain. A white man stopped to see if I was hurt. In several octaves above my natural baritone voice, I squeaked, "I'm fine!" although in fact I could not determine if I felt more physical pain or emotional embarrassment. During the summer of 1955, I was truly an accident waiting to happen.

The Barbershop

But that was last summer. This summer was going to be different. I looked at the clock on the wall. It was nearly 2:30 p.m. I had used up a whole hour daydreaming about last summer. Miss McKayhan told the class that we would spend the remaining hour talking about our plans for the summer. I was sure that I could pay attention for the last hour of school—I was more likely to listen to stuff that I did not actually have to learn. Miss McKayhan called on Raymond to tell the class what he was going to do this summer. Raymond said that he would be working for Mr. Elbert Crisp in the Crisp Barbershop.

Crisp's Barbershop was more than a place for a haircut, shave and a shoeshine; it was a place where colored men could be men; a place where opinions could be expressed freely. It was in some ways an adult community center where men came to give and receive the latest news of the week or day. In Mary and Margie's beauty shop it was called gossip; but in the Crisp Barbershop, it was reporting the latest news of importance to the community. Everyone could have an opinion, whether they got their hair cut, mustache trimmed, face shaved or shoes shined. Skilled hands made fine razor lines along the ears and back of the neck.

The haircuts, trims, shaves, and shoe shines were essential weekly rituals in preparation for the men's roles as leaders in the church on Sunday mornings. Daddy also stopped by the barbershop everyday to catch up on what was happening. Sometimes the men would talk about girls. This was often the mainstay of their conversation. There were Ebony pinups everywhere on the walls. Both the barbers and the customers liked the girls with the big behinds, and most of the posters had girls with such brief bathing suits, there was very little left to the imagination.

Crisp's Barbershop had once belonged to my uncles, Cliff and Bill. My grandfather, William Hennessee, had started the barbershop when he moved to Morganton from Boone, North Carolina. I never knew him. In fact, he died when my mother was only four. Mother was the youngest of eight children—four girls and four boys. My maternal grandfather, William Hennessee, was the son of a white woman and a colored man. He was an adult and a practicing barber when he came to Morganton. Momma told me that she was only 13 when she married William Hennessee, but she also added, "I must have been crazy to marry so young."

Mother said that her father was a skilled barber who had made a good living in Morganton serving a "whites only" clientele. He had his shop in the middle of town; his barbershop did so well he purchased a two-story white clapboard, shuttered house on White Street for his family. They were the first colored family to live in that all-white neighborhood. No one could tell that Momma was colored, but it was evident that William Hennessee was colored or of mixed blood. Judging from photographs of him, his skin was fair, but ruddy. His black hair was almost straight, but not quite. He had a large mustache, and a nose with nostrils that flared. He was a tall, proud, handsome man who provided well for his family. When he died, his oldest boys, Uncle Bill and Uncle Cliff, who also trained as barbers, took over the business. Unfortunately, the Hennessees eventually had to sell the barbershop; and without an income, Momma also lost her house. This devastated my grandmother, who was forced to move into a rented house on the corner of Concord and Anderson Streets.

By the time Elbert Crisp purchased the barbershop, all the white customers had left; so Elbert catered to Negroes only. He hired Cliff as one of his barbers and occasionally one of Cliff's former white customers would come in for a haircut. That was interesting. We could never go into a white barbershop, even when my granddaddy was the barber. Yet, there was no problem for whites to come into a Negro barbershop to get their hair cut.

In the barbershop, the AME Zion minister came up for discussion almost as much as the pretty girls. There was always a problem with the current minister. Most ministers could never satisfy everyone and often ended up satisfying no one. Martin Luther King, Jr., was another primary topic of conversation. Everybody followed the Civil Rights Movement. There was a lot of discussion regarding the *Brown* decision that had come down from the Supreme Court two years before, but nothing had changed in Morganton in 1956. Some of the older men felt that radicals from the North ought to stay out of the South and leave well enough alone. Most, however, took great pride in seeing young men and women challenge segregation.

Elbert Crisp, his brother Willie, my cousin Oliver, and the ministers were the most vocal in support of Civil Rights. These were men who made their living in the black community. Blacks who worked for white people tended to be more conservative in their opinions. Few blacks expressed their true feelings in front of white people. Regardless of what most blacks felt about Dr. King personally, after his house was bombed in Montgomery, Alabama, he became a hero to everyone.

Mr. Crisp always dominated the conversation even when the very opinionated Cliff Hennessee was working. Of the four barber chairs, the owner's chair was most prominent at the end of the shop, next came Cliff's, and then Junior Robinson's (Junior cut hair part time). There was another chair for use by any new barber hired. These new barbers would come to

Morganton for just a year or less. None ever settled in town. The cushioned customer chairs were made of green simulated leather and chrome and sat against the far wall as you entered the barbershop. Over half of the chairs had torn upholstery that Mr. Crisp had repaired with duct tape. The shoeshine stand sat at the end of the row of barber chairs. Here Raymond Brewer worked all summer shining shoes.

I hated to walk into the barbershop when it was filled with customers. That meant that I had to walk past a whole row of men and boys and of course at least one would say, "What's up, Flathead?" Daddy made us get a haircut every two weeks. He made prior arrangements with Mr. Crisp to cut our hair and he would pay for it at the end of the month. He also would tell the barbers how he wanted our hair to be cut. So, when we sat down and asked that the sides be left long or that we wanted a razor cut around the neck, we ended up with the same haircut as usual. This meant that most of the hair was taken off the top and the sides were cut close with no razor cut as per Toots Fleming's instructions!

The barbershop never changed. There were the calendars on the wall next to the state barber licenses. There was a leather strap used to sharpen straight razors. A metal handle was used to raise the barber chairs hydraulically. A child's bolster chair was hanging on the wall. The floor always had balls of hair all over it, usually natural, occasionally mixed with naturally straight, curly, or processed hair. Behind each chair were a sink, a wall mirror, and a little wooden cabinet with a glass door used for storing equipment. A long shelf ran the length of the wall behind the barbers' chairs and under the individual cabinets. The shelf held each barber's special stock of aftershave lotions, pomades, hair oils, powder, and a container of green disinfectant for keeping combs and other items sanitary.

One can learn a lot just by observing and listening in a barbershop. I remember the first time I saw someone get a "process." Before the advent of permanents for Afro-American hair, if a man wanted to straighten his hair he usually got a "process." This consisted of some lye and other unknown ingredients that were made into a paste and plastered all over the head to straighten out the tightly curled natural hair. If this paste were left on too long, it could burn the scalp, and if not left on long enough, it would not do the required job. After fellows had gotten a "process," they were very careful not to get their hair wet. Water could cause the hair to revert to its natural state. If a man with a process got caught in the rain, you could bet your last dollar that he found a cover of some sort to protect his hair. To keep a process straight, a man would wear a "do-rag" or a "Susie." The do-rag would keep the waves and curls in place while sleeping, but it was not unusual to see a man wearing his do-rag during the day. Now, a Susie could be worn with or without a process. "Suzies" were the thigh sections of a lady's stocking cut off below the knee and tied in a knot at the knee-end to create a stocking cap. Pomade grease could create waves in anybody's hair and a Susie was used to keep the wave undisturbed during the night.

Close Encounters

"Frank, will you stop!" That was the second time I had to tell Frank Tucker to stop using his pencil to tickle me behind my ear. The first time this had happened, I had been startled and that made him laugh. So from then on, he thought this annoying little habit was funny. This time it stopped me from daydreaming in class.

By the time I heard what was being said, half the class had already revealed what their plans for the summer were. Tina said that she would care for her brothers and sisters. Ella Mae was going to visit relatives in Washington. Sheila would stay home and look after her younger brothers and sisters at the house. Betty was going to spend the summer in East Orange, New Jersey. I wondered who lived in Orange, if black people lived in East Orange. Steve, whose mother taught the third grade, would have a real vacation of course. As expected, the Williams family was going to go to Key West, Florida. I had never been out of the state, although we did spend many summers at the beach in Camp Lejeune, North Carolina.

My Aunt Em (Emily) and my Uncle Bill (my mother's sister and brother) both lived in Jacksonville, NC, with their families. The Marine base, Camp Lejeune, was in Jacksonville. Aunt Em was a dietician on the base and Uncle Bill was one of the head barbers. They both lived and raised their families in base housing. Aunt Em was as round as she was tall, or so it seemed. She was very light-skinned with black straight hair. She had a crooked smile that gave her an impish look when she laughed. She was always very kind and generous to all her nieces and nephews.

Aunt Em had married Arthur Edmondson from High Point, NC. Arthur was one of the darkest men I knew. Em and Arthur had one son named JW. I never knew what JW stood for. That was his name, so I never asked. JW was a dark chocolate brown with curly, almost straight black hair. He looked like a native of India. I really liked my cousin JW.

When I was only five, JW had taken me to Jacksonville with him on the bus. We had to sit in the back of the bus. JW took the very back seat so that I could stretch out and go to sleep, but it was not easy to sleep in the back near the motor. There was the noise and the smell of the engine. JW said that it was best to sit as far in the back as you could. That way, you were away from white people. He said that some poor whites who rode the bus sometimes looked to make trouble for Negroes. The only problem I had was when we changed buses at Rocky Mount. I forgot my apple and orange and left them on the bus. I felt like I had just lost a hundred dollars, but JW assured me that his mother had plenty of apples and oranges.

That was in 1949. Two years later, JW joined the Marines and at 19 years of age, was shipped off to the Korean War. On a Sunday afternoon in July, 1951, Daddy took us to the Ebony Grill for ice cream. We got word that JW had been killed in action in Korea. Daddy said that he must have been part of the effort to push the Chinese out of Seoul and north of the 38th Parallel. I didn't understand it. We left the grill and immediately drove to Momma's house. Momma, Aunt Annie, Lucille, and Em were all sitting on the front porch in rocking chairs. Mother got out of the car first and went up to her sister to tell her that her son and only child, who could not sit in the front of a bus in North Carolina, had been killed fighting for freedom that his own country denied him. Momma, Aunt Annie, Lucille, and Mother all followed Em into the privacy of the living room after they received the news. I sat on the ground just below the living room windows and listened. My Aunt Emily was inconsolable as she screamed and cried for her only child. My grandmother and the other women of my mother's family also cried and moaned so loudly that I could not help but cry for J.W., too. Their grief that afternoon was overwhelming.

We were too little to go to the funeral. Aunt Lillian kept us and allowed us to walk over to the cemetery for the full military burial and the 21-gun salute. I think we all cried when Aunt Em accepted the United States flag given to her by the officer in charge. Aunt Em was taken back to Momma's house, but she never overcame the heartbreak of JW's death.

After JW died, we often traveled to Jacksonville to visit with Aunt Em. Sometimes we would take cousin David with us. It was a long bus ride, over 350 miles. If we happened to get a local bus, it could take forever. We loved going to Jacksonville. It was like we had run of the Marine base with both my Aunt Em and Uncle Bill working there. With the exception of his daughter Betty Jean, all of Bill's children had left home. Mary Margaret, William, and Corinne were either married or in college. Betty Jean was a young lady who had her own social life and was too busy to spend a lot of time with her young nieces and nephews. Lucky for us, Uncle Bill didn't seem to mind having us around. Sometimes Bill would take us to work with him. Cutting military hair was easy. He just used his clippers and cut all the Marine's hair off. Uncle Bill could cut the hair of 15 men in one hour. He had an automatic shaving lather machine behind his barber chair. Every chance I got, I would push the button and fill my hand full of lather. I wiped the lather on my face and pretended to shave. Uncle Bill would eventually tell me to stop wasting his lather.

Going to the beach was another reason we loved Jacksonville. Aunt Em had plenty of military friends and she had lots of parties. There was never a problem of getting to the beach. Often Aunt Em would plan these elaborate picnics with fried chicken, potato salad, little sandwiches, pickles, cakes, and everything else she could load into a picnic basket. In Camp LeJeune, the Marines had a beach for coloreds and a beach for white Marines. We went to the beach for coloreds.

Anticipation was part of the fun. We would pack everything we needed in two cars. Aunt Em took care of the lunch, and we packed the inner tube, the tire pump, the water mattress, the beach towels, the buckets, and the shovels. From Jacksonville, it was about a 45 minute drive to the colored beach. Not long after we left the base housing, we would find ourselves in the country. You could see the dirt change over to sand. We knew we were getting close. You could smell the ocean miles from the beach. The salt-infused air filled our nostrils with the smell of the sea and added to our anticipation. Finally, we could hear the break of the waves as they hit the sandy shore in front of the sand dunes that still prevented us from actually seeing the ocean. Aunt Em's friends would try to park the car, but we were usually too anxious. Before the cars could come to a complete stop, we would jump out and run toward the water before Mother could caution us not to.

We would run up the dunes, through the Club House, and down the sandy white beach to the water's edge. We would jump up and down in the water with all the excitement of children seeing the ocean for the first time. Mother would have to call us back to help unpack the cars. With the initial thrill passed, we would run back up the beach, through the Club House and down to the parking lot to help unload. Aunt Em usually found a good spot on the patio to set up our gear. The Club House had showers, restrooms, and a bar. Everybody drank beer all day. Occasionally Mother would let us sip her beer. The smell of beer and the sea only added to our exotic adventure.

I will never forget that summer when we kids were five, six and seven. We were having a great time on the beach. Em's Marine friend, Oscar, was playing with us. Oscar was a tall, dark brown man with a thick mustache that hung over his upper lip. He must have lifted weights because he was very muscular. Oscar carried me out into the water on his shoulders with Aunt Em by his side. Aunt Em was as short as Oscar was tall. We were having a great time in the surf. I was on Oscar's shoulders. Wave after wave crashed into his body. Finally, a particularly large wave broke just in front of Oscar, knocking him down and easily washing me off his shoulders into what must have been five feet of water. I was too short for my head to clear the top of the water or for my feet to touch the bottom sand. I could not breathe. I waved my hands and kicked my legs violently, until I felt a large hand grab my right arm and yank me out of the water. I instinctively hung onto Oscar for dear life between coughing and spitting our salty water. I yelled: "Take me home!" Oscar and Aunt Em laughed, but I didn't see what was so funny!

Having had such a close encounter with death, I did not venture back into the water for the rest of the day. Later that same day, we saw one lifeguard, and then another rush out into the ocean. After a few minutes, I saw them bring my Aunt Em back to the beach. They laid her on the sand and tried to resuscitate her. One lifeguard gave her mouth-to-mouth resuscitation, after which she began to violently throw up. An amphibian land/sea boat rushed to shore and took her up the beach to the nearest infirmary. By the time I was 12, I was sure that these two incidents, written indelibly on my mind, were the reasons that I was afraid of the water. For the rest of the summer, I never went wading into water above my knees.

"Johnny, what are your plans for the summer?" Miss McKayhan asked me. She called my name twice before I realized that she was speaking to me. I could only think, "Why did she have to call on me right after Steve Williams finished talking about his exotic vacation plans?" What was I to say, that I was going to spend the summer working for Wilford Carson, plowing fields with a mule, slopping hogs, feeding chickens, and hauling trash? No, I could never just tell the plain and simple unvarnished truth.

So I said, "I will be taking riding lessons for the first part of the summer before going to the beach resort on the coast of North Carolina in August." Why didn't I just say that I was planning a fantastic summer, working and having fun with my cousin Ike? Harry and several others followed me with their vacation plans and then the bell rang.

When the bell rang for the last time during that school year, Miss McKayhan told us to gather all of our belongings and be sure not to leave anything because the school would be thoroughly cleaned during the summer. Then she called all of our names in alphabetical order to come up to pick up our report cards.

"Daniel and Hubert Boggle, Raymond Brewer..." Raymond would have all "A's." He was smart like that. When I heard the name, "Brenda Erwin," I knew that I would be next.

"Johnny Fleming."

"Thank you, Miss McKayhan. I hope you have a good summer."

"You too, Johnny," she said.

I walked out the door, down the hall to the front of the building. Only then, when I was pretty much by myself, did I dare to look at my report card. A row of "C's," punctuated by the occasional "B," mostly for behavior and attendance. A "C-" in spelling – which was actually an improvement! A "C" in arithmetic and a C+ in social studies. I was thankful for no "D's," since Miss McKayhan said I had a problem paying attention in class. All in all, it was not a bad card for me. Not good enough for any rewards, but not bad enough for punishment. After all, I had passed like most of my classmates. So I would think no more about grades, school, or books, or anything until September. I was ready for summer and Ike's arrival.

I would see some of my classmates during the summer, but most of them I would not see. I knew that I would see Raymond at the Barbershop, for example, but my summer would be too busy to see most of my school buddies. I did not expect to go to the movies much this summer because of too many things to do. I went straight to Aunt Lillian's from school. I asked DePapa, "When is Uncle Louie coming?" He said that he thought that they would get to Morganton around noon on Saturday. I couldn't wait!

CHAPTER III:
IKE AND THE ENDLESS SUMMER

Traveling by Car

My grandfather, DePapa, said that Uncle Louie and his family would arrive in Morganton sometime around noon on Saturday. Because they were traveling by car, I knew that their arrival time could not be accurately predicted. My Daddy had a 1951 Plymouth in 1956. We never had a new car and Uncle Louie's cars were usually older and less reliable than Daddy's. We were always several years behind the latest model, but unlike Uncle Louie, Daddy took pride in the way his cars ran and looked. Uncle Joe, who lived part of the year in Philadelphia and part of the year in Durham, where his wife taught school, had the latest and best of everything; at least that's what I assumed, and I'm sure that was the image he wanted to project. His cars were always the same model as the current year. Daddy said that Joe, like a lot of Negroes from the South, rented the latest model car to drive back South to show off how well he was doing up North. Daddy said that some of these Negroes who bought fine new cars had to live in them because they could not afford both a car payment and rent. I did not believe that Uncle Joe was like that. He was married to a teacher! They had the best of everything. Joe, his wife Helen, and their son Joe Berry, all wore tweed suits. Only ministers and teachers wore suits. Joe Berry even wore suits that had matching short pants! Not even Steve Williams, whose mother was a teacher, wore suits.

In 1953 when I was in the third grade, Aunt Helen gave my mother some of Joe Berry's clothes that were too little for him or that were out of style. Among the clothes, I found that she had sent a pair of Joe Berry's knickers. They were the best looking tweed pants I had ever seen and were made out of wool. I had seen people wear them with long socks in some of the old movies from the forties. Some of the kids on the "Little Rascals" wore knickers. I remember the first day I went to school with my knickers and long black socks. Everyone wanted to know where I got "those strange looking pants." I told them, "It's a new style that just hasn't made it to Morganton, but everybody in Philadelphia is wearing them!" I am sure that I was the envy of the class that day. Even though I never saw anyone else wear knickers to school, I liked them anyway.

Every trip that black people took in the United States was an adventure. Even though we knew that North Carolina and every place south was segregated, up north and out west, you never knew where you would be welcomed. It was always hit or miss. You and your family could be terribly humiliated by walking into a restaurant and having the owners say, "We don't serve coloreds here." Daddy told us that sometimes people would reply, "And we don't eat them either!" Somehow it helped to make light of a repressive situation.

Around that time, the American Automobile Association published a pamphlet for middle class Negroes entitled, "Vacation Without Humiliation." The AAA had investigated places of public accommodations that accepted Negro patronage. Armed with that guide, middle class Negroes could safely travel in the North and West without fear of being turned away. There were no integrated eating places in the South. You knew better than to ask if a restaurant served Negroes down South. When black families traveled in the fifties, it was simply a matter of going into a community in the South and asking someone where the black eating establishments were located.

Middle class black people hated to be embarrassed. They were college educated, had good Negro jobs, lived in nice houses, and drove nice cars. They did not play loud music or speak loudly in public places. Their behavior mimicked middle-class white society and they expected a certain level of fair treatment. They were strong supporters of the NAACP through their memberships and cash donations. The NAACP allowed them to protest injustice through legal means that did not jeopardize their jobs.

In the South, where segregation was strictly enforced, you already knew that you were not welcome and would not be served. We did not travel a lot as a family; but we did visit Uncle John and his family in Raleigh, and this was a major trip for us. Even though the trip was less than two hundred miles, it took us the greater part of a day to get there. We would get up early in the morning around 5:00 a.m. and have breakfast. While we finished getting dressed, Mother would pack a lunch, usually fried chicken, sliced white bread, fruit and cake. We always had a one-gallon thermos filled with homemade lemonade. We had to be careful just how much we drank because we never knew where we would be able to stop and use public facilities. We would try to use the restrooms at gas stations. While a few owners would look the other way, most would not allow you to use the restrooms or the restrooms had "Whites only" signs. The "colored" restrooms were usually dirty and smelly. It seemed they were never cleaned. A husband did not want his wife and children exposed to such filth. The woods along the highway were preferable to these unsanitary restrooms.

Driving with Daddy you could never make it to Raleigh without stopping to use the restroom. He drove an average of 40 miles an hour. That by itself would have made the trip long enough, but it did not take into account time spent getting lost. I don't know how well Daddy could read a road map. As we traveled along state route 70 to Raleigh, you had to pay close attention and follow the signs. There was a lot of turning to do, especially in towns that didn't have a bypass.

All of these things contributed to the time it took us to complete our trip. We had to go to the bathroom at least once and sometimes twice. Usually, we would pull over on some isolated road and use the woods. Mother and Patricia would go first, then Jimmy and I. I don't ever remember Daddy having to use the "restroom" where there was no actual restroom. Sometimes when we had to go, Mother and Patricia would go into the woods, but Mother would make me use the area next to the car. If I pretended I did not have to go, she would make me go anyway. I hated the idea of having to pee right in view of a passing car, not to mention that Patricia might also be peeking.

I will never forget that on our last trip to Raleigh, we saw a poor white woman pull up her dress and pull down her panties and pee right under an underpass in plain view of everyone passing by. Black men were not allowed to view white women in these positions. I thought at the time, "If black boys and men have been killed for 'reckless eyeballing' a white woman, what would they do to us for looking at a white woman pee?" These were very real considerations black people had to think about as they planned trips and things I am sure Uncle Louie had already thought about. With that in mind, I went to bed early Friday night feeling fairly certain that Uncle Louie and Ike would get to Morganton safely.

Cousin Ike's Arrival

Saturday morning came quickly. Patricia and I had finished our housework early that Saturday morning, but Jimmy was always slow to get his work done. He was still washing his side of the kitchen cabinets when we heard a car drive up beside DePapa's house. It was cousin Ike (who was actually named Isaac after our great grandfather), Uncle Louie, Aunt Alice, and cousins Donald and Judy at last! Donald was a little older than Jimmy, and Judy was a little younger than Patricia. Ike and I were the same age. Jimmy, Patricia and I ran up to DePapa's house, and then we all sort of held back as we "sized each other up." Daddy and Mother walked up to Aunt Lillian's as Louie was unloading the suitcases. Ike had two suitcases because he was staying for the whole summer. I did not know that Uncle Louie had asked his father, DePapa, and Aunt Lillian if they would keep Ike for the summer. I had heard something about Ike running around with a rough crowd in Durham, but it would be some time before I learned the details of Ike's difficulty.

Aunt Lillian loved family and believed in Southern hospitality. She had the turkey, dressing, rice, sweet potatoes, gravy, greens, and sweat tea for lunch already prepared. Mother had cooked a ham and made homemade rolls. Aunt Lillian planned to serve the same meal for both lunch and dinner. The food stayed on top of the stove all day for those who needed to go back for a snack. Uncle Louie worked hard and ate like a working man, putting more food in his mouth before he had swallowed what was already in there. Aunt Alice was concerned about her figure and did not want to eat a lot of food that would make her gain weight. Donald and Ike ate like growing boys while Judy just messed over her food. Jimmy, Patricia and I all stood around the dinning room table or in the doorways of the living room and kitchen while they ate. We had eaten our lunch at home, so it was just DePapa, Aunt

Lillian, and Tommy who joined our city relatives for lunch.

Uncle Louie was born and raised in Morganton. He was a really nice guy. He was always quiet, had an infectious smile, and worked hard to care for his family. Aunt Alice was born in Durham, the big city. Durham had more black-owned businesses than any other city in the South. Durham was the home of North Carolina College, the state liberal arts college for Negroes. All the best Negro students went to North Carolina College. Durham also had a business school. North Carolina Mutual Insurance Company and the Farmers and Mechanics Bank were located in Durham as well. Aunt Alice was "sophisticated" because she was born and raised in Durham. Her boys had an air about them of being "citified" too. Judy was too young to be anything but sweet little Judy. Ike talked a lot. He knew everything. He sort of reminded me of our Uncle Will – they both liked to take control. That was OK for now. I decided that I would hold back and see what this city boy could show me.

No one had actually told me why Ike was staying the summer in Morganton. I was not yet 12, and it never occurred to me that Ike, who would be 13 before the end of the summer, had already been arrested for stealing. Parents who lived up north would often send their children south to live with their grandparents for the summer. Sometimes these kids were in trouble or were troubled youth who needed the strong hand of relatives who not only survived in a racist South, but also often managed to do quite well with the limited opportunities available to Negroes at that time. The South was too dangerous not to know how to get along with white folks. A reckless eyeball or an intemperate remark might mean a whipping or even a hanging. Parents, the church, and the community all worked together to help young people understand and follow this strict racial etiquette. So just as north-erners sent their children south, Uncle Louie was now sending his "citified" son Ike to live with his grandfather for the summer in a more rural environment. You might say that Ike left the city of Durham for the slower pace and more rural values of Morganton.

June was a great time to be in Morganton. June bugs were everywhere! Jimmy, Patricia, Tommy and I would catch June bugs and tie a long thread to one of their legs and fly them like a kite. We thought that this was great fun and did not worry about the poor one-legged June bugs destined to spend the rest of their lives as cripples, having lost one or more limbs when the centrifugal force of the twirling caused the weight of their bodies to pull away from the leg tethered to the string.

It does not take much to comfort a child. Since some of my older schoolmates regularly found some reason to tease me, I found my comfort in family. There was something very reassuring and satisfying to see all of my relatives sitting in the front yard under the two shade trees. There were DePapa, Aunt Lillian, Uncle Louie, Aunt Alice, Mother and Daddy, Uncle Noah, Aunt Clara, and Cousin Edie (who was named Edith for her grandmother). It seemed they never got tired of talking! DePapa could converse on any subject. He read everything. He had a library in his room full of old books. There was a book on Greek history and one on Greek mythology, but the only book I recognized was the Bible, which DePapa read everyday. Aunt Lillian once told me that Dee Fleming (as he was known in the community) had been an extremely smart child. His father Isaac had been born into slavery in 1855. Isaac's father Alfred had lived to see his freedom and the freedom of his children.

William Thomas Fleming (DePapa), Isaac's son, was born in 1872. William Thomas or Dee learned to read and write and impressed Miss Laura Ervin, who wanted to take him with her and her husband to live in England. The Ervins were a well-to-do family in Burke County and could well afford to live anywhere they wanted. But William Thomas's mother, Edith, would not let him go. Like other black families after the Civil War, the Fleming family faced many difficulties trying to survive in the post Reconstruction South; healthy, smart, male children were a clear asset to their survival.

DePapa loved to talk about history, especially family history. He once told his grandchildren that by all accounts, we should have been named "Avery." The last slaveholder who had owned his father and grandfather was Isaac Avery, who had owned 103 slaves in 1860 at Magnolia Plantation in Burke County, North Carolina. DePapa said that his grandfather had wanted to disassociate himself from his slave master by taking a new name. He chose "Fleming" in honor of a white man who had a reputation for being kind and fair to black people.

Alfred and Isaac (DePapa's grandfather and father) had built their first house on what is now called Burkemont Avenue. It was a small log cabin. As the family grew, they added additional rooms to the home, including the addition of a front porch. DePapa said that his grandfather Alfred used to make a point of sitting on his front porch whenever he saw an Avery pass by, to show that he was now "lord and master" of his own household. DePapa said that his father Isaac did not bother anyone; but when roused, he was a man to be reckoned with.

As a young man, I thought about all the things that my grandfather told me. About what proud men his father and grandfather were. About how slavery had not diminished their self esteem. They knew who they were and were proud to be men of African descent. I also wondered what type of life DePapa would have led had he gone to England with the Ervins. He might have stayed there, gotten married, and then his children and grandchildren (me!) would not have been born. So as I listened on that Saturday evening of Ike's arrival in Morganton to "In the Still of the Night" by the Four Satins on the radio, I quietly thought how lucky we were to have DePapa as our grandfather.

DePapa was a short man in stature, very dark in complexion with snow-white hair and a long mustache. He had very fine features—a small nose and thin lips. His feet were extremely small. He wore a size seven shoe, the same size as I wore as a 12-year-old boy. I was sure that if my feet continued to grow at the same rate they were now, by the time I was grown I would probably wear a size 18!

"Goodnight My Love, Well, It's Time To Go" was the next song we heard in the distance. DePapa called me and Ike to come over to where he was sitting.

Mr. Wilford

DePapa said, "Wilford Carson is looking for two boys to help him out this summer. I told Mr. Wilford that my two grandchildren needed summer employment and that you two would be glad to help him."

Now, Aunt Lillian had already told me that we would be helping Mr. Wilford work this summer. I had no idea that it was really DePapa's decision for me and Ike to work for Mr. Wilford. While this meant we would have real jobs, the arrangements that DePapa had made did not call for us to make real money (although we didn't know this at the time). Also, I was not quite sure what this job would entail. I knew that Mr. Wilford did a lot of stuff around town and around the Carson houses. He farmed land next to the Reverend Carson's house, the land behind his house, and the land below Miss Frankie's house. He worked for the North Carolina State Mental Hospital, but I wasn't sure what he did there. I thought that he must also lay bricks like my grandfather since he always wore overalls with cement splattered all over them.

Mr. Wilford Carson was very dark, like his two sisters. With the exception of John Carson, who was brown like his mother, Miss Lucy, the Carson children were all dark like their father. Mr. Wilford always seemed to be old. His hair was gray. His teeth were stained from chewing tobacco and smoking hand-rolled cigarettes. I am not sure that he ever saw a dentist or went to a doctor. He seldom went to church, but he cut the church's grass each week during the summer and lit the coal furnace early Sunday mornings during the winter to assure that there was heat for Sunday school and church service. Mr. Wilford did not talk much, but when he did, everyone listened. Even with their college educations, John, Lucille, and Esther, Mr. Wilford's siblings, had a lot of respect for Mr. Wilford. When he put his foot down, that was it. Nothing else was said.

The lack of a formal education did not diminish a man's standing in the community if he worked hard, led a respectable life, and cared for his family. Mr. Wilford was a kind, gentle man. I remember one time when I was eight I had ridden to Lenoir, North Carolina (a small neighboring town), with Miss Esther Carson and Mr. Wilford in Miss Esther's car. Miss Esther taught the fifth grade at the colored elementary school in Lenoir. Lenoir was about fifteen miles from Morganton, so Miss Esther stayed in Lenoir all week and traveled to Morganton only on weekends. I sat in the back of the Chevrolet as Mr. Wilford drove Miss Esther back to Lenoir. A car suddenly swerved in front of us, forcing Mr. Wilford to brake quickly and causing me to lunge forward from my seat and hit my Adam's apple against the rim of the back seat. A lump began to appear in the front of my neck. Mr. Wilford grabbed me and rubbed my neck with his rough, wrinkled hands. His touch brought an immediate sense of relief as Miss Esther comforted me. That was the only time that I can remember Mr. Wilford touching me or anyone else.

Mr. Wilford's wife, Miss Hester, ("Aunt Hessie," as we called her) was as "country" as they come. She loved to go barefoot both in the house and outdoors. She also did not like to wear bras, so her heavy bosom sagged into rounded bundles near the top of her apron, which she always wore. Miss Hester was just the nicest lady and was beloved by all. Aunt Hessie was a fine cook, too. She could make the best biscuits in the neighborhood. She sifted her flour mixed with salt and baking powder. Next, she cut in her lard and added cold homemade buttermilk. She quickly mixed these ingredients and shaping the biscuits with her hands, she dropped them onto a greased baking sheet. In 12 minutes, the biscuits were ready to serve and I was always ready to eat them. I loved her biscuits and homemade blackberry jelly. She made biscuits several times a day and never failed to cook her husband hot meals three times a day.

My favorite part of her house was her kitchen. She kept her wood stove long after others in the neighborhood had switched to gas or electric stoves. An enameled white metal table with dark green legs sat in the middle of the kitchen floor, surrounded by four green chairs. Her wooden cabinets were painted white. Her cast iron sink sat below double windows that provided a view of the back of the colored school. Just off of the kitchen was the pantry, where she kept dozens and dozens of jars of canned fruit and vegetables from the garden. Aunt Hessie had a country whine to her voice. Sometimes I felt like her sisters-in-law thought that Wilford had married beneath him because Hester had not finished high school. Of course they would never suggest this to their brother and Hester was too good-natured to notice. Hester usually addressed Mr. Wilford as "Daddy"; or called him "Uncle Wilford" in front of his niece Beverly. Wilford and Hester Carson were very devoted to each other.

Aunt Hessie worked as an assistant cook at the white Morganton High

School. Mondays through Fridays she walked to work in the morning and walked home in the afternoon. She and Mother finished their workdays around 2:30 in the afternoon. Sometimes Mother would walk over to Hester's house, where they would sit and talk in the front yard. Sometimes they would sit on the front porch on the green metal porch furniture, the type that graced most homes in the 1950s. Hester had a wonderful wooden swing, thickly textured from its annual coat of green paint, which hung sideways on her front porch. There was a large fig tree growing on the side of Miss Hessie's porch behind the swing; the tree had been rooted years ago from the fig tree on the side of Aunt Lillian's and DePapa's house.

In the back of the house was Mr. Wilford's chicken coop. Miss Hester gathered eggs everyday, but only killed a hen or rooster for Sunday dinner or a special occasion. Everyone knew how to kill and clean a chicken, but not everyone used the same method. My father liked to wring a chicken's neck. This he would accomplish by taking the head of the chicken in his hand and quickly swinging the chicken around and around, breaking the neck by suddenly popping it. Miss Hester preferred to chop off the head of the chicken with an ax. I once saw our neighbor, Mr. Gaither, place a chicken's head between two sticks on the ground and holding the sticks in place with his feet, pull the feet of the chicken until its head popped off. But whatever method was used to kill the chicken, it would always flop around the yard for several minutes (headless!) like it was still alive. As small children we marveled at how the chicken could still move with blood gushing out of a hole where its head once was. It almost appeared as if the frantic chicken were trying to get revenge by spraying blood all over the back yard and on anyone who did not have enough sense to stand back.

The Carsons' garden lay behind their chicken coop and was planted mainly in feed corn. The garden stretched all the way back to the two-horse barn at the end of his property. The double pigpen was situated between the chicken coop and the barn. The pigpen was a low structure, no more than four feet high, and was made out of wood with spaces in between for fresh air to flow. The top of the pen was covered with tin. At the front of the pen was the trough. The pig could poke his neck out through a hole and eat the slop dropped in the trough each night. Dotted throughout the Carson property were fruit trees and vines—apple, pear, muscadines, grapes, and peaches. The only cherry tree in the neighborhood was in the back of Reverend Carson's (Mr. Wilford's father's) house next door to DePapa and Aunt Lillian's house.

One summer evening, when we were about seven, eight, and nine, Jimmy, Patricia and I decided that we wanted some of those deliciously looking bright red cherries. We sneaked across the fence that divided our land from the Carsons', walked gingerly along the fence, and quickly ran over to the cherry tree which stood in the middle of the Carsons' back yard, and unknown to us, were quite visible from the Carsons' kitchen window. We climbed the tree and ate and ate and ate. For some reason, though we still had not eaten "enough," we began to have second thoughts about raiding the Carsons' cherry tree. Unlike the cherry tree that stood in the open yard, the grapevine we also helped ourselves to was on the side of the Carson house and close to the path that we used to go out to our Uncle Will's house. We had gotten used to being able to walk by the grapevine and grab a bunch of grapes without anyone noticing.

Jimmy said, "Somebody is gonna see!"

I came up with a brilliant idea! "Let's go ask if we can have some cherries! That way we can get a bag and pick as many as we want."

"Yeah, I'm tired of eating cherries now, but I might want some later! Let's take some home." Patricia added.

So rather than continuing to risk getting caught, we all agreed that we would ask if we could have some cherries. We boldly walked up to the Carsons' back door and knocked. Miss Lucille came to the door.

We asked very innocently, "May we please have some cherries?" to which Miss Lucille promptly replied, "Haven't you stolen enough for one day?" And to that response, we sheepishly walked back to our house.

This was our neighborhood and the Carsons were our neighbors. Now Mr. Wilford would be our employer. We would start work on Monday at 6:00 a.m., the day after Louie and the rest of Ike's Family left to return to Durham. I stayed at Aunt Lillian's that Sunday night. Both Ike and I slept upstairs in the twin iron beds. (I never would have stayed upstairs alone! Too scary!) Even when there was someone else sharing the room, I preferred to use the "slop jar" at night rather than risk encountering someone or something in the stairwell on the way to the bathroom on the first floor.

Not many people stayed upstairs at DePapa and Aunt Lillian's house after Big Momma died. Big Momma had had the front bedroom that had double windows overlooking Concord Street. There was one full-sized bed in the room. Aunt Lillian often used the room to winter her geraniums because of the sunlight from the south. The third bedroom was now used for storage. This was my sister's favorite room. Patricia often rambled around the room to see what treasures she could find.

The Work Day Begins

"Johnny! Ike! Time to get up!" I heard Aunt Lillian yell from the bottom of the stairs. She woke us up at 5:15 a.m. to make sure that we were dressed and ready to go to work. She prepared breakfast for everyone except Tommy, who was still asleep. DePapa was up and dressed as if he, too, were preparing for a hard day's work. DePapa had been retired for a number of years, but he still got up at the same time every morning. Aunt Lillian had a big pot of coffee ready. The metal coffee pot was still a bright shiny silver even after sitting on top of that stove for decades. It was the type that would perk only after the water boiled and would continue to perk until taken off of direct heat. That pot made some strong coffee!

I didn't know how long the coffee had been on, but it sure smelled good and strong. I had never tasted coffee black. DePapa liked lots of sugar and cream in his coffee. The milkman had already delivered two quarts of milk. Aunt Lillian opened a bottle where the cream had risen to the top and gently poured the cream into a small pitcher. DePapa was already drinking his coffee when Ike and I came downstairs. I pulled a chair up to the table where Aunt Lillian had my coffee waiting. To my Mother's consternation, Aunt Lillian had been giving us coffee ever since we were old enough to ask for it. I put in a whole four teaspoons of sugar and some cream. I stirred the coffee and poured some in my saucer, blowing gently over the saucer before taking a great big gulp. I said, "Aaaahhhhh, that's good" just like I heard DePapa say on so many mornings. Sometime he would drink his coffee with a spoon, but only if he had time to savor it.

We did not have that luxury this morning, so I poured my coffee into the saucer and waited for the bacon, eggs, and toast. Aunt Lillian no longer put our bread on top of the wood stove to brown. She had a new electric toaster with two side compartments. The bread was placed on the door and secured by a metal holder. When the door to the toaster was closed, the elements "electrically" toasted the bread. "Ping!" the toaster would sound when the toast was ready. Aunt Lillian prepared a hearty meal for us, knowing that we would have a long day ahead of us. While I had worked at jobs like cutting grass or looking after kids, I had never worked from sunup to sundown. So, she fortified us with a good breakfast, and we were ready for a day's hard work.

It was a cool, crisp morning. The dew glistened on the grass and slowly dripped from the long smooth magnolia tree leaves. The summer sun was already above the horizon, but had not evaporated the low-lying clouds that continued to hover above Pine Mountain to the south of town. Mr. Wilford was already waiting in his pale green and off white pickup truck. Upon seeing us, he said, "Come on, boys. I'm already late."

Mr. Wilford did not talk much. He never took the time to explain to us what we would be doing for the rest of the summer or, for that matter, even for the rest of the day. While we might have questions and wanted answers, Mr. Wilford had time for neither. To him, it was simple—he would tell us what needed to be done and we would do it and that was that. He barely carried on a conversation with his wife; why we expected him to treat us any differently, I do not know. It was not long before we just accepted Mr. Wilford for who and how he was.

We had no idea what was in store for us. Everyday was a new adventure. Ike said, "Mr. Wilford, can we ride in the back of the truck?" "Yes, but don't stand up," was his only reply. Running around to the back of the pickup truck, Ike said, "Come on, Johnny, get in!" as he pulled the metal pins which held the tailgate up. Up onto the flatbed we scrambled. This was great! "Oh, I always wanted to ride in the back of a truck!" I said. We were free! Mr. Wilford backed out onto Concord Street and drove toward town. The wind blowing in our faces was an indication of the freedom we would experience during the summer. For the first time in over a year, I was happy.

Mr. Wilford's routine seldom varied. His days were marked by constant work. I never knew Mr. Wilford to take a vacation or even to go fishing. He did hunt during the late fall and early winter months. He and my Uncle Will kept hound dogs just for hunting. I suppose that they could have been considered guard dogs, but they were always tied up close to their little wooden doghouses. Next to the dog houses were pots full of fresh water and empty bowls to hold the dog food that consisted mainly of what was left over from dinner with a little dry dog food mixed in. The area around the dog compound consisted of bare earth where the dogs had walked back and forth playing with each other or vying for human attention. The dogs were placed on chains just long enough for some contact, but not too long so that they wouldn't become entangled in the chains. These were animals that loved to hunt, yet they seemed satisfied to live eight months a year tied up by their dog houses until late fall or early winter, when they had a chance to roam the forest looking for rabbits. Hunting must have been in their blood because they did not get to keep the rabbits, only retrieve them once they were shot.

Mr. Wilford was very generous with his bounty. Each year he would deliver several rabbits to our door. He would always skin them and clean the guts out before giving them to Mother or Daddy. He would knock lightly on our back door and hand two rabbits over to Mother and simply say, "Here's two rabbits for you and Toots." Everything Mr. Wilford did, he did quietly and without fuss. Mother could make the best rabbit stew by dousing the rabbits in flour that had been salted and peppered. Then she fried them until they were brown. She placed the browned rabbit pieces into a covered pan, added water, and baked them until tender. They were delicious, even if one accidentally managed to chew down on a bit of buckshot. Even in relaxation, Mr. Wilford served his neighbors.

Mr. Wilford worked at Broughton Hospital as a brick mason. He was a permanent employee, but did not work full-time. He only worked and got paid when some masonry had to be repaired or there was a building project under way. He always wore coveralls, just like DePapa did when he worked. It was at Broughton that DePapa's daddy and my great grandfather, Isaac, learned to lay brick. Aunt Lillian told me that Isaac was very industrious and had wanted to be a good provider for his family. Because Isaac (who had been born into slavery) was still a young boy when slavery ended, he had not been scarred as badly as his father, Alfred, who had lived most of his life in bondage. While Alfred had little tolerance for white people, Isaac could work with anyone. He was a real go-getter. When he learned that work was available at the new hospital for the mentally ill, he was right there applying for a job.

Of course all of the good jobs went to white men, but Isaac was hired as a common laborer to fetch bricks for the white masons. One day Isaac decided that he would try his hand at laying brick. He caught on quickly. Upon returning from lunch, one of the white brick masons saw Isaac laying brick and yelled, "Nigger, what do you think you are doing?! Don't you know that's white man's work?" Isaac stood straight up and looked the man in the eye, but never said a word.

The foreman, "old man Harbison," witnessed the incident and told the white brick mason that he would handle the situation. Then Mr. Harbison saw that Isaac had a talent for laying brick and showed him how to get the exact amount of mortar on his trowel. As long as construction continued at the hospital, Isaac had steady work. The white men did not like Isaac working along side of them. They resented having a "nigger" do "white man's work." In time, though, they saw that Isaac worked hard and did good work, so they let him be.

Aunt Lillian said that Isaac taught his father, Alfred, how to lay brick and later his son, William Thomas (DePapa). Of DePapa's children, only Louis learned the trade and made a living by laying brick. Very few jobs would welcome the threesome because they were in competition with white men. Isaac decided that they should specialize in constructing chimneys since none of the white masons liked that type of work. Building a chimney was highly specialized work. DePapa told me that many of the old southern homes had as many as four flues for the fireplaces connected to the chimney. It was very important to get each flue to draw just right or the smoke would back up into the house. Not many brick masons wanted to spend weeks constructing a chimney, only to have it not work properly. If it did not work, the chimney had to be torn down. But DePapa and Isaac were good, and their work was in demand as far away as Asheville, NC. Aunt Lillian said that DePapa would walk over 50 miles to Asheville to work and would stay there until the job was done.

As much as I loved my granddaddy, I hated going to work with him. One summer DePapa was working on a cinder block foundation off Burkemont Avenue in Morganton, and he needed some laborers to help carry cinder blocks to where he was laying the foundation. Once the cement was mixed, the masons had to work continuously to use all the cement before it dried out. The mixer had to know just how much to mix based upon the number of men laying brick. Even in his mid 70s, DePapa still could lay brick as fast as the youngest man on the job. Daddy made Jimmy and me go with DePapa to carry the cinder blocks for him. He laid cinder blocks faster than the two of us could carry them to him. The gray blocks were about 18 inches long and about half that in width and height; and they were divided into two sections for added strength.

DePapa would carefully but quickly scoop up just the right amount of cement on his trowel and place it on the bottom edges of the block. Then he would add mortar to the edge of the block and put it into place, nudging it with the handle of his trowel until the block was in perfect alignment with the top of the string that was used to ensure a straight row. Of course Jimmy and I were slackers. It was the middle of July and it was hot! There was a qualitative difference between hauling bricks in the midday heat or playing "cowboys and Indians" in the fields back of the colored cemetery.

DePapa had made a good living as a brick mason. His wife did not have to work outside of the home. They raised ten children. Louie, the only one of their children who decided to follow DePapa's lead and lay brick for a living, was good at his work, but when he got an opportunity to work at Liggett and Myers Tobacco Company in Durham, he took the factory job. It may not have paid more, but it was a relatively clean, indoor occupation. Will tried to lay brick for a while, but Will never took any job too seriously or for very long. I doubt that Daddy ever even tried. I know that Uncle John got as far away from this type of work as possible. I can't say that I blame any of them. By the time Jimmy and I finished work that day, we, too, were convinced that we were not cut out to be brick masons and definitely did not want to be common laborers hauling brick all day.

Mr. Wilford did not mind hard work and long hours. I believed that if he could not work, he would quickly die. On the other hand, Uncle Will thought work would kill him and did all that he could to avoid it.

Uncle Will

Uncle Will was what people called "a character." He was always around, not having a steady job other than keeping up with what was happening in the neighborhood and anything else of interest around town. (It would be Will who was the first to discover the goat man traveling through the county.)

Will had married Esther Avery and together they had three boys. James was the oldest, then Mickey, then Charles. They all lived in a small house that had an outhouse in back. Will and Esther's bedroom was to the left of the living room. The three boys all slept together in the second bedroom that was located off the kitchen. Although Will rarely had a steady job, Esther worked full time as a cook for the Rainbow Inn in downtown Morganton. I never knew too much about the Rainbow Inn, since coloreds were not allowed in the Inn except to cook and clean. Esther had to be at work at 1:00 p.m. and worked until after 10:00 at night. She worked from the time she got up in the morning until the time she went to bed at night. We were born on the same day. When I was little, I would give her a 15-cents bottle of finger nail polish for her birthday and she would give me a pair of socks for mine.

I always liked my Aunt Esther. She was a kind, gentle woman. The only time I heard her raise her voice was to yell at Will for something he did not do or more likely, something he did that he should not have. Esther was a stout, brown-skinned woman with fine features and a pleasing manner. She must have been attractive in her day, for you could still see her beauty that often surfaced above her usual state of exhaustion. Will did little to help around the house. Esther tried to maintain a clean house, even with four males of varying ages living there. She would rise in the morning and wash, if needed, before fixing breakfast. After feeding her crew, she would hang her wash out to dry on a clothesline that stretched from the house to the pecan tree in the middle of the backyard. On a summer day, Esther's clothes would be dry before she had to leave for work, giving her time to gather and fold them. During the winter, she often had to leave her clothes on the line, and sometimes they froze before she had a chance to take them in.

By the time she finished her laundry, she still had to clean the house and start the fire for dinner. She also cooked on a wood-burning stove. The family ate their main meal at noon because Esther had to be at work by 1:00 p.m.

Will would not fix his own dinner and usually would hang around DePapa and Aunt Lillian's house near suppertime, hoping to eat dinner with them. If left to his own devices, he was capable of putting some souse meat between saltine crackers and opening an orange soda to drink.

When Will was not hanging around Aunt Lillian's house, he sat on his front porch, watching and waiting for something to happen so that he could report on it. Will was the first to report on the stranger moving through town with his herd of goats. At the time, no one paid any attention to Will's story because it seemed insignificant. Will told Lillian that a dark-skinned white man was traveling across the state with a herd of goats. As it turned out, the man was traveling in a little wagon and herding about 50-60 goats. Each day Will would bring everyone up to date on his progress through the county. Will said that some people started to blame the "goat man" for anything missing or stolen.

Generally, once or twice a week Will would give me or my brother, Jimmy, a nickel to go to either Wallace's or Wall's store to buy him some Prince Albert chewing tobacco. The stores were across the street from each other on Burkemont Avenue, and just two long blocks from where we lived. White people owned them both, but I preferred to give my business to Wall's. The Walls lived next door to the little store they owned. Miss Wall ran the store, while her husband owned and operated the Wall Lumber Company. Miss Wall was a middle-aged white woman who was nice to all of her customers, regardless of race.

Near the front of the store was a glass-fronted cabinet full of the things children want and can afford to buy, that is, "penny candy." My favorite candy was the package of "Kits." I think they were my favorites because you got four "kits" to a pack and each pack only cost a penny. My next favorite was the "BB Bat," which was hard caramel on a stick. It lasted forever, but if you were not careful, it would pull your teeth right out! So, my appreciation of candies was based on the amount of candy and how long it lasted. Miss Walls was as courteous to us as if we were spending dollars, not pennies.

Jimmy and I had to cut our own grass at home, and we learned how to cut grass by hanging around with Will. Will had a lawnmower, which he used to earn money by cutting lawns, sometimes. I don't know what he did in the wintertime when he was not out hunting, but he cut grass in the summertime and this made enough money to buy his tobacco and other necessities, but not enough to raise a family—Esther did that. Yet in spite of everything, we all liked Will. He was OK. He was always there. Will could sit and talk all day long, interrupted only by the need to gather and disseminate news on a regular basis.

Will was also funny and quite self-sufficient. One evening, having had a little too much to drink, he fell off his front porch, (two steps above the ground) and broke his arm. He took aspirins that evening for the pain. The next day, he went to the Morganton Hardware store and purchased some plaster of Paris. He tore up an old pillowcase for bandages and soaked them in the plaster of parish mixture. To set his arm, he tied a rope to his hand and wrapped the other end around a porch post and pulled the rope with his good hand until he heard the bone snap into place! He quickly wrapped it in the soaked plaster of Paris bandages. The bandages hardened to form a cast. Four weeks later, he removed the self-made cast and his arm had completely healed, even though it was crooked.

We would never have thought of Will as knowing how to dance, but he could. One day we were playing at Aunt Lillian's when Will walked in. We were trying to learn the latest dance, as Will sat down to watch. Will was just in his late 40s, but looked much older because he was short and heavy set. He wore coveralls, which made him look even more rotund. When Will suggested that we could learn a few dance steps from him, we all laughed. The laughter must have challenged Will because he got up and started to perform a dance that looked like a combination of a two-step, the chicken, and a buck dance.

He gathered his pants legs up to just above the ankles to expose his brogan enclosed feet. As heavy as Will was, he showed a remarkable degree of agility as he "jitterbugged" about the floor, gliding to and fro to musical tunes he remembered from the 1940s. Jimmy, Patricia, Tommy and I fell out laughing, but that did not stop Uncle Will. While he probably had not danced in 20 years, it was obvious he had never forgotten how.

Aunt Lillian said that when Will had been a young man in his early 20s, he'd left Morganton and moved to Durham. When they finally heard from Will, he had married a very rich woman named Margaret Peters, who was in her 60s. We always heard, but Aunt Lillian did not actually say, that Miss Peters/Fleming was a "woman of the world." We gathered that she was experienced and worldly. Will was her fourth husband. Her former husbands were all well-to-do and left Miss Peters well off. If she married older men for their money, she certainly must have married Will for his youth and looks because he did not have any money. Aunt Lillian said that when he was married to Mrs. Peters, Will had stepchildren twice his age. Will told us that those were the "good old days" when he had a suit for every day in the week. Aunt Lillian told us that Will's stepchildren were opposed to the marriage and Will and Miss Margaret Peters were soon separated. In spite of all of Will's experiences, he was still likeable, even if we were admonished not to follow his example.

The Work Day

DePapa had a role model in mind when he arranged for Ike to live in Morganton for the summer, and Mr. Wilford was definitely it. I thought this was a little extreme because all Mr. Wilford did was work! Mr. Wilford did not talk much, so at the beginning, we did not know what we would be doing from day to day or sometimes even hour to hour. We soon learned what our workday was like. He told us what to do and we did it. Then he would tell us something else to do and we did that, too. This went on until quitting time.

Mr. Wilford took us to Broughton's Hospital on our first day even though he was not laying brick. He made his early morning run to collect garbage for his dogs. We would return to the hospital in the late afternoon to collect slop for his hogs. Now, I could not really tell the difference between "garbage" for the dogs and "slop" for the hogs, except that we would add a little dry dog food to the dogs' dinners and the hogs got what they got, with no additives. This stuff was free and allowed Mr. Wilford to maintain eight dogs and two hogs. He had a horse, but he didn't get any provisions for the horse from Broughton's.

Ike and I loaded the buckets with the leftovers from breakfast at the hospital and put them in the back of the truck. This time we climbed into the cab to ride. While the breakfast run wasn't so bad, nobody wanted to sit in the back of the truck with slop sloshing around, and it didn't matter whether it was for the dogs or hogs. Mr. Wilford pulled into his driveway and drove halfway down the slope where the hound compounds were located. He stopped the truck. Ike and I got out and unloaded the buckets. We mixed the garbage with dry dog food and gave each dog a share. We got the garden hose and provided fresh water for each dog. As we went about our work, the hounds all barked and jumped, each wanting our attention, a pat on the head, or a rub on the back. Mr. Wilford only said, "Shut up," as he kept moving.

We walked down to the barn where the horse was housed. None of Mr. Wilford's animals had names. They were "the hound dogs," "the pigs," "the horse," and "the goats." Miss Hester called the goats "Billy" even though they were both females, but she didn't have names for the other animals.

The barn, which was at the very end of the long narrow yard, lay adjacent to the Olive Hill schoolyard. Mr. Wilford's yard ran south from Concord Street parallel to the schoolyard and the cemetery. Mr. Wilford's back yard sloped downhill while the cemetery lay uphill from his small horse barn. The barn had two doors and was fronted by a corral. The horse was allowed to come in and out of the barn as he wished during the day, but was shut up inside at night. Mr. Wilford showed us how to use a shovel to clean out the manure from the barn floor and the corral. We had to pile the manure next to the barn for future use. It generated so much heat that in the fall and winter, you could see smoke rising from the pile! He showed us where the clean hay was located and how to place a layer of hay over the floor of the barn. We also placed a stack of hay in the corner of the corral where the horse fed. We had to go way back up the hill to where the hose was to get the horse fresh water. Ike and I both carried a five gallon container of water for the horse up to the barn. We would do this twice each day.

We did not have to feed the goats. We just moved the stake that they were tied to and their water dish to a new location that had plenty of fresh grass for the goats to eat. But we had to be careful not to put them in an area that had wild onions. Mr. Wilford's goats were milking goats and he did not want their milk to taste like wild onions. The milk smelled bad enough as it was! I know that Mr. Wilford drank goat's milk, as did my Daddy. Mr. Wilford would send Daddy a gallon container of milk once a week. Daddy drank most of it. I tried to drink it, but I could never develop a taste for goat's milk. Once Daddy complained that his milk tasted like wild onions. I am sure that was the day we had chained the goats too close to Miss Hessie's garden where the wild onions grew. But, Mr. Wilford never asked about it, and we did not volunteer any information.

Once the morning chores were done, we prepared the horse for plowing. We spent the rest of the day and the next plowing the Carsons' fields and the neighbors' garden plots. We also helped plow the long and narrow field behind Mr. Wilford's house. After that we plowed the garden next to Reverend Carsons' house that separated my Uncle Will's property from the Rev. Carson's property. Mr. John Carson and his wife, Miss Frankie, wanted the land below their house plowed so that Mr. Wilford could plant a crop there. Mr. Wilford also plowed DePapa's garden and Will's garden. While DePapa kept a wonderful weed free garden throughout the summer, by August it was difficult to tell vegetable from weed in Will's garden.

Mr. Wilford showed us how to place the bit in the horse's mouth, put the harness over the horse, and hook the horse to the plow. He showed us how to hang onto the rein and to use the rein to make the horse move forward, turn to the left or right, and stop. That first day Mr. Wilford did most of the plowing, but let us take turns holding the plow in front of him. The horse moved in a steady, slow movement up the hill and then down, creating furrows of dirt that would turn the weeds over while not disturbing the young corn stalks. Mr. Wilford had planted his corn in the field below his house earlier in the season. This corn would serve as feed for his chickens and supplement the hay given to his horse. All the corn had been planted in May and was not quite knee high in June. We had had a warm, wet spring, which gave the crops a head start on what was predicted to be a long and somewhat dry summer. All morning long June bugs surrounded us. I could not remember so many June bugs so early in the year. I asked Ike if he knew how to fly a June bug. He said "no," and I said that I would teach him.

We stopped at noon for lunch. We ate at Mr. Wilford's house. Miss Hester had fried pork chops, okra, and corn, and was making biscuits as we walked into the kitchen. As usual, Miss Hester made making biscuits look simple. Within 12 minutes, we had piping hot, golden brown, buttermilk biscuits with some of her homemade pear preserves. What a great meal!

Ike was not used to eating like this. While his mother had been born in the South, it was "city South." She did not cook heavy meals for lunch. During the summer when the kids were at home, she generally prepared soup and sandwiches for lunch. Ike said that they ate Campbell soup, all the time.

"After that big breakfast Aunt Lillian fixed, I thought I would not eat again until supper!" he added. He was wrong. After the workout Mr. Wilford had given us, we both were starving. We both had seconds on the pork chops and corn. I don't think Ike was used to eating okra, but that would change during his summer in Morganton. Two helpings of biscuits and pear preserves served as our dessert and completed our meal. We washed everything down with a large glass of cold buttermilk that had specks of real butter still floating in it.

It took the rest of the afternoon and into the evening to complete plowing the field. Mr. Wilford showed us how to wash down the horse to cool it off and dry it before walking it back to the barn. We provided additional hay and water, but this time we put the feed inside the barn and locked the horse up for the night. Later, when Mr. Wilford trusted me and Ike to do this by ourselves, this would be the highlight of the day because we would ride the horse back to the stable, rather than walk him. Riding that horse compensated for all of the hard work during the day. We would take turns riding. It was like playing an Indian in a western movie. (We had to be Indians because only Indians rode bareback. I don't think Mr. Wilford even owned a saddle.)

After putting the horse in the barn, we drove back to the State Hospital to collect the slop for the hogs. On the way back, we stopped by Miss Lucille's and

Miss Esther's (Mr. Wilford's sisters who lived with his father Rev. Carson) to collect whatever slop they had accumulated during the day and placed it, too, on the truck bed. The Carsons always kept a large five-gallon bucket next to the back steps. After each meal, they would scrape any leftover food into the bucket. Everything went into that bucket—coffee, juice, eggs, bacon, bread, peels from fruit—it didn't matter. Once no one wanted the leftovers, the leftovers became hog food. With the buckets of slop, we drove down to the hog pen, where we emptied the buckets into the hog troughs. We watched the hogs make pigs out of themselves, covering their snouts with the thick mixture of the residue from hundreds of meals. We watered the pigs, dogs, and goats, and headed home too tired to think about eating ourselves.

The Runaways

We went to bed early that first evening, knowing that we would have to rise early the next morning. But still, we talked for a while.

"Why do you want to be a minister?" Ike asked.

"What kind of question is that? Is there something wrong with being a minister?" I replied somewhat defensively. While becoming a minister was my life-long goal, more than anything I wanted to be accepted. I dreaded the notion that someone might identify me as being different.

Ike thought for a moment, "You know, Johnny, I got into some trouble down in Durham before school was over. I don't know what it is about me, but I always end up doing something wrong."

I said, "Nobody is perfect. I get into trouble all the time. Why, last year, my Mother told me that if I did one more thing wrong at school, she was going to quit her job!"

Ike became more attentive. "What did you do?" he asked.

"Well, it all started with me and David running away from home."

"You guys actually ran away from home!" Ike exclaimed.

I told Ike the long story. "It all began with television, I think."

"Television?" Ike said puzzled.

"Yes," I continued. "Sometimes we would see these TV shows where kids run away from home. I think the first time I heard of a kid running away might have been on the 'Little Rascals.' We watched them all the time. Jimmy, David, and I always thought that running away would be an adventure. But we never thought that we would have a reason to actually run away."

"Well, last year around May, David came over to my house just before school. He told me that he was tired of being punished by Aunt Annie. She locked him in the closet or made him get under the bed for the least little incident. David and I had talked before about Momma and Aunt Annie getting old. In fact we talked about how hard it would be on us if any of our older relatives died. I said that I could not bear the thought of Mother or Aunt Lillian dying. I would rather die myself. Aunt Annie and Momma, who are both over 70 years old, take care of David. David has lived with them all of his life, but David hated to be punished by them all of the time.

"You know David never knew his mother. She died when he was only six months old. Well, after his mother died, Momma went to Washington and brought him back to Morganton. Even at her age, she took David in to raise him like her own son. Everybody said that David had a heart problem, but nobody said what that problem was."

Ike asked, "Is David my cousin?"

"No, he's my mother's sister Annie Margaret's son."

I continued the story. "So we started comparing notes about all the reasons why we should run away from home. I, of course, felt like I had all the reasons in the world to leave home. Daddy's not like what we thought a daddy should be. He's nothing like the dads on 'Father Knows Best' or 'Ozzie and Harriet.' Daddy's always there to punish us when we misbehave, but he never does anything with us. It is hard to love a person who punishes you all the time. I was tired of getting whippings, too. So, David and I decided that we did not have to take their punishments any more. We sat there and began to figure out our plan of action.

"We decided that we would run away from home that very day. We would go to school and act normal. We would return home at noon. It being lunch hour, we would have an hour to get out of town before we would be missed. We met at my house. We always kept our camping gear, which we had purchased from the Army/Navy Store, packed and ready to use. We kept our cooking utensils in our knapsacks with the knife and canteen. To this we added Vienna sausage, potted meat, pork and beans, and other canned goods. I got my Bible and wrote Mother and Daddy a note. I simply said that I was tired of being whipped all the time and that I was going to run away. I loved Mother and told her not to worry about me. I would be fine. I left the note on top of the television. And then we left."

Ike asked, "Did you have a plan? Where were you going? Did you have any money?"

"Don't rush me, Ike. I'm going to tell you everything!" I said. "We decided to head north and double back in case anyone saw us leave because that maneuver would throw them off our trail. We walked north past Mr. Gaither's house onto Burkemont Avenue. Then we proceeded west out Burkemont Avenue until we got to the train tracks. At the bridge, we climbed down the hill to the tracks and started walking east. We walked by the depot until it was out of sight. Just before the track made a sharp turn to the south, we decided to rest. We must have walked a couple of miles and thought that this would be a good place to hop a train since we didn't have much money. We reasoned that the train would stop at the depot and being a freight train, it would be moving at a slow speed. Our plan was to catch the first freight train that came by. We decided that the train would take us to Greensboro, where we would get off. We would find our cousin Sarah Mae, who lived in Greensboro. Mother had stayed with her several times when she was taking summer courses for dieticians at North Carolina A & T College. We would live with Sarah Mae. That was our solution even though neither of us could think of her last name. We would just find her.

"David and I decided to sit under a shade tree while we waited for the train. I pulled out my Bible and started reading it. After awhile, David said, 'Johnny, look up. Who is that coming down the track?' I was really disappointed when I looked up and saw my Brother Jimmy and his friend Harry Corpening walking down the train track. I thought we had covered our tracks pretty good. We sat there until they came up and asked us what we were doing. Jimmy said that after lunch our teachers reported us missing to the principal, Mr. Morris, and that Mr. Morris immediately notified Mother in the cafeteria. Jimmy and Harry were recruited to look for us. Jimmy said that the whole school was talking about us, being missing and all. No one could remember anyone ever running away. We were hot news!

"Jimmy said that he remembered our habit of hanging around the tracks and our talk about one day catching a freight train. So, he figured that the first thing we would do is head for the train tracks. He said that they were just about to stop looking for us and head back, but then they had seen two people sitting under a tree and decided to investigate. I thought to myself that if only we had waited until after we passed the sharp turn to stop and rest, they never would have seen us.

"David said that he was not going back. I thought about it and figured that since Jimmy and Harry caught us this time, they could find us again once they went back to school to give their report. So, I told David that we might as well go back and he finally agreed.

"Ike, I can't tell you how hard it was to make the decision to go home. My own brother thought I was crazy!

"We went back to school and were taken to Mr. Morris's office where he questioned us."

"What did he say? Did he whip you?" Ike anxiously asked.

"No, he didn't whip us! Mr. Morris kept asking the same question, over and over, 'Why did you boys run off like that?'

"I knew why; but I could not tell Mr. Morris. I just kept saying over and over, 'I dunno, I dunno.' "

"What happened then?"

"Mr. Morris expelled us both from school. We went to my house, where I unpacked my knapsack. Since Mother had not seen the note I had left on top of the television, I picked it up and put it in my pocket. I wondered where Mother was, since she obviously had not seen the note. David and I walked outside and saw Mother sitting in the front yard of Hester Carson. We walked over there and Mother started asking us a lot of questions to which we had no real answers. She told David that he should go home because Momma was worried about him. I went home to my room. When Daddy came home, Mother told him what had happened. He became angry and told me to get the strap. He beat me as he usually did until welts appeared on my arms and legs. The whipping I received was part of the reason why I ran away, but I did not tell him that.

"Well, Mother had to go to see Mr. Morris to get me back in school. Do you ever seem to stay in trouble? Like, no matter what you do, it is wrong?"

I asked Ike.

"Johnny, you know me. I am always doing something wrong or saying the wrong thing. But I never ran away from home!" he added.

"I don't think a week passed before we were in trouble again. It's not that we meant to do anything wrong, it's just that we did not think about the consequences. How did I know I would be expelled from school again in a week's time?"

"What did you do?"

"Well, David and I were just messing around the school – throwing rocks, breaking milk bottles – you know, the 'usual stuff.' We walked up to the back of the school and looked through the basement window where the coach keeps all the football equipment and the sodas. I guess we wanted a soda. We cut the wire to the screen over the window, but it turned out the window was locked. But, we knew better than to break the window!

"We went home that night and did not think anymore about it. The next day, Mr. Morris called each of us into his office and questioned us separately. David broke under pressure and admitted that we did it. Mr. Morris said for us to go on home and that we could not come back until our parents had met with him.

"Mother was at school when she was called to the principal's office. She was mad! When Daddy came home, he got mad too. But this time he did not beat me. Mother told him and me that if she was called into the Principal's office one more time, she was going to quit her job! While I thought that this was a little drastic, I took her seriously and vowed that I would try to get through the end of the year without getting into any more trouble. Daddy told me to go outside and help DePapa and Aunt Lillian in the garden, which I did. Neither DePapa nor Aunt Lillian said anything to me. We just pulled weeds.

"Ike, I tell you, last year was the worst year of my life! I became known as the 'Runaway.' No matter where I went or who saw me, everyone labeled me as 'Runaway.' I hated it. It was worse than being called 'Flathead!' Last year was just awful."

Ike said, "Wow, thanks for telling me. I guess that I am not the only bad boy in this family."

Ike and I soon fell asleep. We had bonded and were the best of friends for the rest of the summer.

My paternal grandfather William Thomas Fleming "DePapa" (on the far right)
with his sister, Clara F. Holloway, and his brother, John Fleming on the
porch of DePapa's house in Morganton, North Carolina.

My maternal grandmother Mary Margaret Hennessee (on the far right) with her mother and siblings. From left to right: Charles Woodard, Cora Perry, Annie Woodward, Great Grandmother Emily Crisp Woodard, and Edward Woodard.

My grandmother Margaret, Great Grandmother Emily,
Mother Mary holding my sister, Patricia Emily, summer of 1946.

Dad, Mother and their friend
Tim Erwin during a Sunday afternoon car trip.

Family photograph of my paternal grandparents, their children and
grandchildren taken during the celebration of their 50th wedding anniversary.
Standing from right to left: Aunt Lillian Fleming, Uncle Ernest Fleming, Uncle
George Fleming and his wife Rita, my father James Fleming, my mother Mary
Fleming, Uncle Joseph Fleming and his wife Helen, Uncle Louis Fleming and
his wife Alice (Ike's parents). Seated from left to right: My Grandmother Rebecca
is holding my brother Jimmy, DePapa is holding me, and standing between
my grandparents are cousins Joe Berry and Leilani.

My maternal Aunts Annie Margaret and Lucille Hennessee with their sister-in-law Rheupert Hennessee.

My maternal Aunt Emily (Em) H. Edmondson.

Patricia Fleming, Jimmy Fleming, and Johnny Fleming (author) in the fall of 1946 in front of Olive Hill School.

Johnny, Jimmy and Patricia in 1949.

My cousin J.W. Edmondson (my Aunt Emily's only child) in his U.S. Marines uniform prior to going to Korea in 1951.

Aunt Hortense (my Uncle John's wife) and their son Sundar in 1950.

Cousin David Hennessee on his front porch with his bicycle.

Uncle John following his graduation from Oberlin College in Ohio

Cousin Tommy Tapp, and Lillian F. Tapp. My favorite Aunt.

Olive Hill School
(Courtesy of Burke County Library)

DePapa's House with the wisteria vine in the tree in front.
The Carson's house is on the right with Daddy's car in the driveway.

The front yard was a favorite gathering
place in the evening for family and friends.

Sundar Fleming's 5th Birthday Party in Raleigh, North Carolina, c. 1955.
Sundar is standing on the front row to the right of the birthday cake.
Ike is standing on the back row to the left of Sundar.

Wilford Carson as a young man
(Courtesy of Doris Young)

Wilford's wife Hester Carson.
(Courtesy of Doris Young)

School Photos

Mother (Mary Fleming)
was the dietician for Olive Hill School.

Patricia Fleming in the fifth grade.

Jimmy Fleming
in the seventh grade.

Johnny Fleming
in the sixth grade.

Classmates

Courtesy of Linda Williams Fleming, Brenda Erwin Brewer, Margarite Morris, Francis Corpening Elliott, and Effie Mae Willi

Linda Williams

Raymond Brewer

Brenda Erwin

Wilhelmina Paige

Steve Williams

Margarite Morris

Francis Corpening

Sunday School at Slades Chapel AME Zion Church
(Courtesy of Burke County Library)

Senior Choir at Slades Chapel. DePapa is on the second row, last person on the right
(Courtesy of Burke County Library)

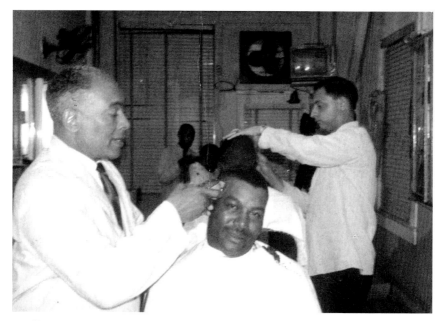

Elbert Crisp (standing on the left) in the Crisp Barber Shop on East Union Street.
Elbert hired my brother Jimmy (standing on the right) after he finished barber school.
(Courtesy of Burke County Library)

The Avery Building at Broughton Hospital. My great grandfather
Isaac learned to lay brick at Broughton; Wilford Carson also worked at Broughton.
(Courtesy of Burke County Library)

The Mimosa Theater. The colored section was
down the alley and up the interior stairs.
(Courtesy of Burke County Library)

Union Street downtown looking toward the
West. Union Street was the main Street in town.
(Wayne Hitt, Courtesy of Burke County Library)

The Caldwell Hotel. In the background, lower
left is Slades Chapel. Blacks worked in the
Hotel but were not served as customers.
(Courtesy of Burke County Library).

The Train Depot. When David and Johnny ran away from home,
they passed the depot where they planned to catch a train to Greensboro.
(Courtesy of Burke County Library)

Johnny in front of Olive Hill School reflecting on the summer of 1956.

CHAPTER IV:
SUMMER TIME

Vacation Bible School

Mr. Wilford's routine did not vary from day to day. Sometimes the only way we could tell one day from another depended on such simple things as where we picked up the slop. On Mondays, Wednesdays, and Fridays, we picked up slop from the State Hospital; on Tuesdays, Thursdays, and Saturdays, slop was collected from the State School for the Deaf. Each summer day passed swiftly. June was almost over! It was already the last Sunday in June. Evening had come and the family assumed its traditional place in the front yard under the shade trees heavy with blooming wisteria, where we waited for the evening's first cool breeze.

DePapa said, "Vacation Bible School starts at Slades Chapel on Monday morning. Gaither Perkins will take you children and pick you up everyday. You should be ready by 8:30 tomorrow morning."

DePapa never asked if you wanted to do anything; he just made an announcement. "Go to bed." "Pull weeds." "Go to church." And now it was,

"Go to Vacation Bible School!"

Vacation Bible School would ruin Mr. Wilford's work schedule for Ike and me; and even worse, we would have to go every morning for a solid week! How would Mr. Wilford get along without us? But when we told him that we could work only in the afternoons, he did not seem terribly upset. Of course, Mr. Wilford was a member of Slades Chapel.

Slades Chapel AME (African Methodist Episcopal) Zion Church was established after the Civil War. Aunt Lillian said that her grandfather Isaac and great, grandfather Alfred were founding members of the Church. Black communities throughout the South established two institutions: churches and schools. Many churches like Slades Chapel functioned as both religious institutions and educational institutions. Colored families came together, pooled their resources and labor to construct the church. Slades Chapel, founded in 1881, grew out of Gaston Chapel, organized in 1868. The first minister was Reverend Mayhue Slade.

DePapa said, "They observed Sunday just like the Israelites. When I was a child, we were not allowed to play; we could only go to church. 'Sunday' was observed all day: there were morning services, which included Sunday school, then church, followed by a break for the mid-day meal, with church resuming for the afternoon service."

As soon as churches were established, schools quickly followed. Aunt Lillian said that her grandfather, Isaac, remembered the Freedmen's Bureau, which helped establish schools for the newly-freed slaves. Some sympathetic whites also helped establish schools such as the Kistler Academy, named for its founder A.M. Kistler. You would often find in those classes a mix of men, women, girls, and boys. After slavery, everyone wanted to learn how to read and write. Adults most often attended night school, because they had to work during the day. No sacrifice was too great to make for the sake of education.

During slavery, blacks had been prohibited from learning how to read and write. After emancipation when former slaves were given the opportunity to learn to read and write, everyone old and young took advantage of schooling.

Slades Chapel AME Zion Church and Gaston Chapel AME Church were important institutions in Morganton. Aunt Lillian said that these churches were the heart of the black community. At a time when welfare did not exist, these churches provided spiritual comfort and material support for their members. Children were born into the church but were not baptized until they could make a free-will choice to dedicate their lives to Christ. They joined the church, attended Sunday school and church services, Bible classes, and Bible School. They joined the choir, the usher board, the missionary society; they became elders, deacons; they married in the church, aided the sick and elderly, and were finally buried in the church.

When I thought about the things DePapa and Aunt Lillian told me, I realized how significant Slades Chapel had been to both the Fleming family and the Carson family. I began to understand why Mr. Wilford did not question our absence from work so long as we were going to Bible School at Slades Chapel.

As we sat in the front yard that Sunday evening, Will came around the corner of the house and asked in an excited voice, "Has anyone heard that someone broke into Miss Mae Lee's house and took a chicken and some potatoes right off the stove?"

Dad asked, "Did she call the police?"

Still very much excited, Will explained, "Well, they didn't actually break into the house. The back door was unlocked and Miss Mae Lee was sitting on the front porch. She didn't hear or see anything until she went into the house to finish cooking her dinner. Then she discovered the chicken and potatoes were missing from the top of the stove!" Only Will connected the missing food with the Tates' pies, gone missing the week before. No one else saw the connection.

As Ike and I sat on the front steps of DePapa's house, we were more concerned with the news Aunt Lillian had than with the news just reported by Will. We heard Aunt Lillian tell Mother and Daddy that Mr. Gaither would take us to Bible School—Jimmy, Patricia, Tommy, Beverly Carson, Ike and I. We were to be at his house at 8:30 a.m. sharp.

Mr. Gaither's house was in back of the Reverend Carson's house between West Concord Street and Burkemont Avenue. All the houses on Burkemont Avenue were occupied by whites. And, nearly all the families at the end of Concord Street where we lived were black. The white families on Concord Street did not really live on Concord. Their houses abutted the street but actually faced Circle Court, which intersected with Concord. So blacks and whites lived side by side, but remained total strangers. They did not bother us and we did not bother them. We didn't even know the names of the poor white families who lived behind our house.

Ike said, "Hey Johnny, come over here, me and Jimmy got a plan."

I had not seen Jimmy and Ike move from DePapa's front porch to the front porch of our house. I quietly moved over to them and said, "OK, what's the plan?"

Ike said, "We're planning to skip Vacation Bible School." He continued, "Tomorrow, we're gonna get dressed and pretend to walk out to Mr. Gaither's, but instead we're gonna cut across the Carsons' yard and then down by the front of Will's house. That way, we can spend the whole day playing in the hollow."

Ike, new to the area, was already intrigued by the legends of the hollow. "We'll dam up the stream down in the hollow and make us a swimming pool!" The hollow was such a great place to play. There was always something to see and do in the hollow in spite of Miss Mae Lee always yelling, "Get out of that hollow! You will make my house cave in!"

Her house never did cave in on us, so we generally ignored Miss Mae Lee and continued our adventures in the hollow. Sometimes we would stand at the front of the "bear cave" and dare that bear to come out. We were convinced that bears were in there, and despite Aunt Lucille's warnings of bears eating bad children, we felt it was only a matter of time before we found that bear and his family. Sometimes if we were really adventurous, we might crawl in on our hands and knees, but we never moved far enough into the cave where we could not see the light. And while we never actually saw bears there, we never gave up our belief that if we investigated that cave long enough, we would find the bears.

But we never got to the hollow that following Monday. We all got up bright and early that morning and met at Aunt Lillian's house. We left the house as a group through the side door, passed across the Carsons' backyard and headed toward Mr. Gaither's house. Rather than go through the gate leading to Mr. Gaither's house, we quickly ran past the Carsons' utility house and jumped the fence in front of Will's yard. As we sped past the front of Will's house and down his driveway leading to Concord Street, we looked up to see our grandfather DePapa suddenly appear out of nowhere at the end of the drive.

We nearly peed in our pants when we saw him looming at the end of the drive with his chain-gang whip in his hand. Our shock immediately turned to desperation. We instinctively turned on our heels and sprinted with all our might back up the hill where we turned toward Aunt Lillian's house. Along the side of the house we moved cautiously. We quietly walked to the front yard and saw DePapa coming up the street. He still had the chain-gang whip in his hands. (Aunt Lillian had told us that DePapa had gotten that whip from a white man who worked as a guard on the chain gang.)

All of his children at one time or another had told us that DePapa was a no-nonsense father. He ruled his household with a firm hand. He knew that he had to be strict with his boys because he understood the problems of trying to raise young black boys during the early 1900s in a southern town that would be unforgiving to those who made the mistake of breaking racial etiquette. He believed in the "Spare the rod and spoil the child" philosophy. Aunt Lillian said that when her daddy got that whip, it had had a leather handle with several dozen thin strips and each strip had a metal tip. "Momma got very upset when Papa bought that whip home," she said. "As a concession to Momma, he cut each of the metal tips off the leather strips."

Daddy had said that his Papa knew how to punish a child. "Most of the time Papa was late getting home from work, but even when he arrived on time, he would not whip you right away. No sir, Papa waited until we had gone to bed. Then he would slowly walk up the stairs and across the wooden floors. If we were awake, it was agony awaiting each step as he moved closer and closer to our room. But if we were asleep, as we often were, we would not hear Papa enter into our room. And before we knew anything, Papa would pull the covers back, raise his arm with the whip in hand and start in to whippin' us!"

He continued, "You can well imagine the immediate fright from being awakened from a deep sleep with the pain of a chain-gang whip descending on your partially naked bodies."

But Daddy must not have thought it was so bad, because he practiced the same method of punishment. Many were the times he would come home and pull our covers back to whip Jimmy or me for some wrong we had done during the day. Of course Jimmy, and Patricia and I had our part of the whipping ritual down pat.

As soon as it became evident that we were going to get a whipping, we would start crying. It would take a moment for the real tears to start flowing down our cheeks as we shifted from side to side, one foot to the other. As Daddy would move closer, we would scream louder, reaching an incredibly high pitch by the time he grabbed us with one hand while his other arm lowered the strap that had been sliced in several places to spread the pain.

With the first lash, Daddy would start his litany. "Why did you do that?" The whip would pop!

"Didn't I tell you not to do that?" Pop!

"So why did you do that?" Pop!

Agonizingly slow and laborious, he would start, "Are you " (Pop!) "going to do it again?" Pop! Pop!

By this time we would be yelling at the top of our voices, "I ain't going to do it no more! I ain't never going to do it no more!" The routine was always the same, no matter what "it" was, we were adamant that we would never do it again! He would have us by one hand, beating us with the other, while we wiggled around trying to gain our freedom and scooting around on one leg trying to encircle him as though this forward movement would help us escape the next lash of the strap or at least lessen its impact as we moved.

We thought that if we cried and yelled loud enough, it would be a sure sign that the whipping was having an impact, that we were learning our lesson, and that we certainly would not do it again. We also hoped in vain that such outbursts would gain the sympathy of Mother, who seldom if ever whipped us. But in fact, she would usually go to another room while all this "carrying on" was going on. Later, we would show her the welts that the strap had caused on our arms and legs. Mother would get out the rubbing alcohol and gently massage our arms and legs. I am not sure that the alcohol helped, but her gentle touch surely felt good and gave us comfort. Mother never said or gave any impression that she disagreed with our being whipped. In fact most of the time, it was she who had to tell Daddy about the infraction, unless he heard it from a neighbor first, which made it worse.

So, here was DePapa chasing us with the same whip that he had used to beat his own children and he did not care who knew it. In fact, one time when I was about eight, I had been especially bad. Aunt Lillian could take a lot from us children, but this particular day I was just plain mean. Aunt Lillian finally put me out of her house. Boy, was I mad! I started banging on the front door. It was a wooden frame door with three rows of three glass panes; three across and three down. Aunt Lillian had sheer curtains over the glass to keep people from looking in while allowing her to see who was at the door. I banged and then started kicking the door, when all of a sudden DePapa came to the door and asked, "What's wrong with you, boy? You want me to give you a whippin'?"

Already beginning to cry, I said, "You can't whip me! I'll tell my Daddy on you!"

But DePapa replied, "Go ahead, tell your Daddy. I will whip you AND your Daddy."

That's all the information I needed that day to go on home. Anyone bold enough to take on my Daddy must have been mean!

DePapa had never actually whipped any of us as far as I can remember. Yet, for a short man, he was a commanding figure. He had the voice of authority, and now, the whip he held in his hands as he walked up Concord Street reinforced his authority. Like Supermen, we ran like the wind, first back toward Aunt Lillian's house, then around to the side past the weeping willow that divided our house from DePapa's house. DePapa's age had no bearing on how fast he could run. We could not shake him. We ran faster! We passed the pear tree and cut sharply around the east corner of our house, down a gentle slope that was still wet from the morning dew. I glanced over my left shoulder to see that DePapa was still hot on our trail. Jimmy was in front, then Ike, and I was behind. Jimmy successfully made the slippery ninety-degree turn around the northwest corner of the house, followed by Ike. But as I turned the corner, my feet flew out from under me on the wet grass. As quickly as I attempted to get up, I felt the metal-less tips of the straps fall heavily on my back.

DePapa stood over me and yelled, "Get up!"

I received one blow of the lash, but it might as well have been 20! The tears began to roll down my cheeks. I was in pain! First, from the humiliation of having fallen, as if still living up to the name, "Clumsy," and then, from the agony of knowing that Jimmy and Ike had seen me fall and get the lash. It was bad enough being beaten, without having witnesses to my humiliation! And finally, the actual lash itself given to me by my grandfather hurt my feelings and pride more than my body. DePapa had never whipped any of us before.

"Get up," DePapa again ordered. He marched me into Aunt Lillian's house, where she washed my face and dried my clothes with a towel. DePapa walked into the dinning room and said, "Let's go!"

I walked slowly out the side door, followed by DePapa. We retraced our earlier steps across the Carsons' back yard, but this time, we continued through the gate into Mr. Gaither's yard. And there were Jimmy, Tommy, Beverly, Patricia, and Ike all sitting in the car! Embarrassed, I got into the car and we drove off to Vacation Bible School.

We sat in the car quietly. No one said a word. DePapa once again had proven to everyone who was head of the Fleming Family. He was never challenged. I never told Daddy what happened, but he must have known. We never talked about it because even as a grown man, my father did not challenge his father. He knew that he had been whipped with the same whip.

Vacation Bible School turned out to be not all that bad. We gathered in the basement of the church for assembly. We usually sang a few hymns like "Jesus Loves Me, Yes I Know," "Go Tell It on the Mountain," or "Jesus Wants Me to be a Sunbeam." (This song was for the younger children.) Someone would be asked to say the morning prayer. If the minister were present, he would come in and give us a few words of wisdom. There would be announcements of the day's activities, especially if we were going to take a little fieldtrip or if someone special was coming in before noon to speak to us children.

We broke up into smaller groups based on age. Ike and I were in the upper middle group. Miss Annie Fullwood was our teacher. Miss Fullwood worked for Burand's Department Store in Morganton. She was a very religious lady and would take four vacation days from work to teach the Bible School Class. Everybody liked Miss Fullwood, even Ike. Therefore, we took this class seriously and studied our lessons as if we were in regular school.

Mr. Flemon F. McIntosh was the Superintendent of Vacation Bible School. He taught math classes to the high school students at Olive Hill School and coached the football team. He was a large man who gave the impression of authority. His wife, Nettie McGimpsey, was also a school teacher who coordinated the logistics for school programs. Nettie McGimpsey was related to the Hennessees, my mother's side of the family, but I was never sure just how. Despite the fact that he had only recently graduated from college, Mr. McIntosh had already assumed a leadership role in the community. You always knew that he was in charge.

This summer was certainly unlike the Bible School of three years ago that had been held at Gaston Chapel. At that time, I was with the younger students who were hard to control. I was always getting in trouble and seemed to never stop talking. Mr. McIntosh, the Superintendent of Vacation Bible School, always placed regular schoolteachers over unruly classes. That summer, Miss Barber was our teacher. Miss Barber was my daddy's first cousin and my second cousin. We still called her "Miss Barber," though, even though her name was Helen. She was quiet and seemed easy to ignore. We talked and laughed and had a good time in her class, or so I thought.

Everything had been going fine until "The Spider Incident." While using the bathroom, I noticed a large, black, dead spider on the bathroom floor of the Church basement. I gently scooped up the spider with a piece of toilet paper, which I carefully wrapped around the spider before placing it in my shirt pocket. While I had no immediate need for the spider, it was always a good idea to take advantage of what was available at the time, not knowing when the need might arise for a dead black spider. Sure enough, no sooner had I returned to Bible class than I saw an opportunity. There sat Linda Williams, who was always afraid of everything, especially bugs. When we were in the third grade, a helicopter had flown over the school, making a lot of noise and obviously disrupting the class. Miss Effie Williams, the mother of my best friend, Steve Williams, who was Linda's aunt by marriage, asked Linda what was making all of that noise. Linda had replied, "A big black bug." The whole class laughed out loud.

So the girl who three years ago thought that the helicopter was a big black bug was now about to face the real thing. Turning my back to Linda, I unwrapped the toilet paper from around the spider and ever so quietly, I gently placed the spider on Linda arm. Now, Linda was always known for being a little more dramatic than circumstances required, but I could never have imagined the star performance she would give that day.

I touched her arm as if to suggest movement of the spider. She turned, looked at her arm, and shock moved across her face. She tried to scream, but there was no sound. I thought, "This is really going to be a good performance!" She was actually screaming without sound! Finally, in seconds that seemed like eternity, the scream, lodged in her stomach, began to move forward up her throat. With a great big push from her diaphragm, her mouth opened and she let loose a most horrible scream, which grabbed everybody's attention. I tried to pretend that I was as surprised as everyone else. Miss Barber came over quickly and asked what had happened. Linda said, "Joohnyyy Joohnyyy ppuuttt, ppuuttt a a a sspiider on, on me!" Miss Barber turned around and slapped my face as hard as she could. I was momentarily stunned. I had never been hit like that before, so I was shocked into silence. I sat down quietly and said nothing for the rest of the day.

When we got home, Jimmy told Mother what had happened. Still shaken, I tried to deny it. "She did not!" So, Mother asked me again, "Did Helen Barber slap you in the face?" I meekly said, "Yes."

Immediately Mother went to the phone and called Miss Barber. I heard her ask Helen if she had slapped me. Evidently, from the response of my mother, Helen had said "Yes." I had never seen Mother so angry. She told Helen that she was never to put her hands on me or any of her other children. After that, we were always kind of cool toward Miss Helen Barber despite the fact that she was my father's first cousin.

The French Kiss

Nothing as eventful as "the spider and the slap" happened for the remainder of the week in Vacation Bible School. While we attended Vacation Bible School, there was a routine that we followed religiously. Each day, we generally ended at noon with a sandwich, a cookie, and Kool Aid. The ladies of the Church prepared the sandwiches and they were usually peanut butter, cheese, or bologna, always on day-old Sunbeam bread donated by the bakery. Ike and I ate our lunches quickly because we had to get home to change into our work clothes and head over to Mr. Wilford's.

On the last day of Vacation Bible School, I was sick and missed the little closing ceremony. Shortly past noon, after he changed his clothes, Ike came by the house to bring me my certificate of attendance. Ike said that he and Mr. Wilford were headed to Bridgewater. They were going to spend the day in the country working on Miss Hester's old home place. Miss Annie, Aunt Hessie's sister, still lived on the place, but Mr. Wilford took care of the grounds and farmed the land.

By dusk, I was feeling better. My stomach did not hurt and my diarrhea was gone. I anxiously waited for Ike to come home and tell me about his day in Bridgewater. Finally he came, long after we had finished dinner. We sat on the back porch and he told me of his exploits in the country.

"I met Frances up there in the country," he said, "Frances Wilkins." Now, Frances was an older woman, already 13 and going into the eight grade. She knew everything there was to know about love and sex. She was taller than Ike. She had long dark hair and cocoa brown skin with freckles. She had large full lips, which she painted red when her mother was not around. Whatever we talked about, the conversation usually ended up in some form of competition. Ike said, "Frances gives the best French kiss I've ever had."

Before I could figure out what a "French kiss" was, I blurted out "I bet I had a better French kiss from Ella Mae!" completely ignoring the fact that I hadn't kissed Ella Mae since we were six years old. It would never have occurred to Ike, raised in the city, that I hadn't kissed a girl since kissing Ella Mae in the first grade.

Ike said, "Johnny, you're wrong this time. Frances can REALLY kiss!

You don't know what tongue is until you kiss Frances!"

"Tongue?" I thought to myself. "What does 'tongue' have to do with kissing?"

"Look, Johnny, we are going back up to Bridgewater on Monday. Frances lives next door to Miss Annie's. So you'll have a chance to kiss Frances and see what I mean."

All night I dreamed about the mystery woman named Frances. I would get my first French kiss and learn about this tongue thing all at the same time. Of course I had only kissed girls on the cheek. I could not now remember what it felt like when I had kissed Ella Mae on the lips, because it had been so long since we were in the first grade.

Yet, in the first grade I had believed that I was in love with Ella Mae, otherwise, why would I have given her a piece of my mother's jewelry? I still remember roaming through Mother's jewelry box, looking for something a first grader would want. I found a brooch that I wrapped in notebook paper and sealed it with tape. I wrote "Ella Mae" on the front, but did not write my name. I sat next to Ella Mae in class and when she was not looking, it was simple enough for me to put this little package under her desk in the compartment designed for books. When she finally found and opened my little package, she stared at it. I realize now that she must have thought, "Why would anyone put a woman's brooch under my seat?" How would I know a six-year-old didn't wear brooches? Ella Mae turned my gift in to the teacher without ever knowing that the brooch was a token of my love for her.

The next day, I got up still wondering what was different about this French kissing?

I got dressed and stopped at Aunt Lillian's to pick up Ike. Mr. Wilford had already loaded his truck and was waiting for us. We hurriedly completed our morning chores of feeding and watering the animals. We would not return until nightfall. We could not ride in the back today because Mr. Wilford had loaded cement, sand, buckets, and a wheelbarrow on the bed of the truck. We asked, "What are we going to do today?" and Mr. Wilford replied that we had to replace Miss Annie's old, worn out, wooden porch with a cement one. He and Ike had removed the old porch the day before on Saturday. Our job was to collect pieces of brick and stones to made a base for the cement. This took all morning.

Then we had the lunch that Frances and her mother brought to us. Mrs. Wilkins lived next door to Miss Annie. I thought that they were related in some way, but I was not sure. Frances did not talk to me and Ike while in the presence of her mother. They had fixed our plates—fried whole catfish, coleslaw, corn bread, and fried okra with buttermilk to drink. Boy, that food was good! Even Ike had at last come around to liking okra. We certainly ate enough of it that summer.

We washed our hands with water from the garden hose. Without soap, all we could do was rinse off the worst of the dirt and cement. We ate heartedly. Mr. Wilford sat quietly and ate his food without saying a word. Then he sat under the nearby oak tree, pulled out his can of Prince Albert tobacco and his sheets of cigarette papers, and proceeded to roll a cigarette. He placed the thin, white paper between his left thumb and index finger and poured the tobacco directly onto the paper with his right hand. He slowly rolled the paper until there was just under a quarter inch exposed. He licked the length of the exposed paper and sealed the cigarette. He pulled a box of wooden matches from his overalls and lit the cigarette. He found great pleasure not only in smoking the cigarette, but also in the process of making it.

After he finished, he said that it was time to start mixing the cement. We pulled the large cement bags from the truck while Mr. Wilford shoveled the sand into the wheelbarrow. We filled several buckets with water and added the ingredients to a flat, cement encrusted, wooden trough where we would mix the water, cement, and sand until just the right consistency. Mr. Wilford determined when that was. Ike and I then shoveled the cement mixture back into the wheelbarrow, hauled the mixture to the porch and up a plank incline, where we unloaded the mixture into the waiting forms. We carried load after load until Mr. Wilford said, "That's enough!" It was getting late and he wanted to smooth out the mixture while we cleaned the tools.

We hurriedly completed the job because we saw Frances sitting on her porch next door. We casually walked toward her house, keeping an eye out for Mr. Wilford and another one out for Frances' mother, Miss Wilkins. Frances told us to follow her around to the side of the house. Ike and Frances starting kissing and hugging while I stood there. She gave him deep, long kisses. When she stopped, she walked over to me and pressing her full red lips into mine, she PUT HER TONGUE IN MY MOUTH! I nearly choked. I felt the warm, almost hot, moist, smooth tongue move around my mouth as if searching for something it had lost.

Her red lip firmly pressed against mine. I had never felt anything quite like this before. Kissing Ella Mae was what kids did. This was the "real thing!" I was hot all over. I never wanted that moment to end.

"Frances!"

"Frances, where are you?" Miss Wilkins yelled again. "It's getting dark and it's time for you to come on in."

Frances quickly pulled her tongue from my mouth and abruptly said, "I gotta go."

She walked around to the front porch and quietly watched as Ike and I loaded Mr. Wilford's trowel, level, and gloves onto the truck. I said, "Frances sure can kiss!" and Ike smiled and said, "Didn't I tell you?"

Blackberries

The next week was short because of the July 4th weekend, making work even more demanding. While Mr. Wilford would not take the day off, he was determined that if we took the holiday, we had to make up the time we missed. By July 1st, we surely were ready for an extended weekend. This was going to be a special week, what with the community picnic and my sister Patricia's birthday on the 2nd.

Each time I think about birthdays, I still think about parties. It's funny because I never had a real party. Jimmy had a party when he was in the first grade. Mother allowed him to invite all of his little first grade friends to the house. I will never forget that cold rainy day on February 19th. We did not do much. Just played in our room, had little party hats and cake and ice cream. What made it different from other birthdays was that guests were invited! Jimmy got presents, lots of presents. From that moment on, I associated all birthdays (especially my birthdays) with parties. Every year I invited anyone I saw to come to my birthday party. Mother, if she heard, would immediately say that I was not having a party. What that meant to me was that I was not having a birthday. I knew that wasn't true, so I continued telling everyone to come to my party. I don't know why Mother didn't understand that birthdays and parties were the same.

That Monday, both Ike and I returned exhausted from another long day of hard work, I went home and Ike went on up to Aunt Lillian's. Mother had already prepared dinner and everyone had eaten except me. Everything on the table had come right out of the garden—the sweet corn had been cut from the cob and creamed, the okra had been sautéed in butter, the tomatoes were stewed with bread, onion and a little sugar. There was one pork chop left and a quarter of a pan of corn bread on the stove. I washed up and ate alone at the kitchen table.

As I ate, I looked around the room and noticed that the kitchen cabinets had been washed. I thought to myself, "Ha ha, Jimmy had to do that job by himself." We never got paid for work we did around the house. Every Saturday Mother and Daddy laid out a series of chores that we had to do before we could go outside or turn on the TV. That was a great incentive, especially when we wanted to see our favorite programs. From the time that we were little we had had to do chores, from simple dusting to mopping and vacuuming the floors. We all hated washing the windows and the kitchen cabinets. I think it was because of the awkward physical positions, stretching and bending, those jobs required. Our windows had endless little panes, six horizontal rows of three panes each. We would first wash them with vinegar and water and then we would wipe and wipe and wipe. They always seemed to streak, no matter what we did.

Washing the kitchen cabinets was another one of those jobs that had to be done three to four times a year, more if company was coming over. It was important for Mother to have a clean kitchen, where so much entertaining took place. It was a great place to talk. While not a large kitchen, especially with the laminated metal table in the middle of the floor, it was a warm and inviting place. The refrigerator was on the right as you entered the kitchen from the living room; there were twin windows that looked out toward Aunt Lillian's house and the garden in back. The kitchen sink sat below the windows. Since we had hot water only on Wednesdays and Saturdays when Daddy lit the hot water heater for our semi-weekly baths, all other times we had to heat water on the stove. Daddy was thrifty. We were the only people I knew who heated their water with kerosene. Most of the time the heater stayed off. Daddy had figured out how long in advance of the first bath he needed to light the water heater to have sufficient hot water for everyone to bathe. If one went beyond his time limit for bathing, the last person or even the second-to-last person to bathe would not have enough hot water. The kerosene heater would have to stay on for another half hour and Daddy would have to stay up to turn it off.

It was not just the hot water – Daddy was thrifty with everything. He would buy three-way light bulbs that seemed to us to be a mere 25, 30, and 35 watts. Even if the bulb was using only 25 watts, he would make you go back into a room to make sure you turned off the only lamp left in the room. I used to think, "When I have my own home, the one thing it will be is well-lit!"

The city had not extended the gas line to our neighborhood, so we had to use bottled gas for the stove. The stove was placed opposite the refrigerator and next to the back door. So, "washing the kitchen cabinets" really meant that we not only had to clean them, but also wash down the refrigerator and the stove and then mop the kitchen. Patricia never had to do any of this, but she did have to wash the dishes and that she did every day. I remember the first time Mother asked us kids to wash the dishes. Well, she really did not ask us, she told Jimmy that he would have to wash the dishes since he was the oldest and did not have to stand on one of the little chairs to reach the sink. We each had a little chair we sat on to watch television at night. Jimmy had an armless chair with a hand woven seat. My chair was slightly smaller than Jimmy's with arms on each side. Patricia's chair had arms and rockers.

At first we were all excited over doing an adult job like washing the dishes, and the first couple of times, Jimmy was excited, too. He used this as an example of the privileges that come with being the oldest child. But he soon learned that washing dishes was drudgery and his interest in the job was reflected by the amount of food left on the plates after washing. Mother tried to work with Jimmy, but he could never do them to her satisfaction. Soon Patricia was promoted to "number one dishwasher." Even though she had to stand on Jimmy's chair, a perfect platform from which to wash the dishes, she did a much better job in getting the dishes clean.

As I sat alone finishing dinner in the kitchen, Mother came in and told me to put my dishes in the sink and she would fix me some of her fresh blackberry pie. Mother was an excellent pie maker and her blackberry pie was exceptional. The main reason her pies were so good was the flaky crust she knew how to make. Plus, these were blackberries Jimmy and Patricia had picked earlier in June.

I still laugh when I think about when Daddy had come home one Friday evening and told Jimmy and Patricia to get their things ready because he was taking them to the country to pick blackberries first thing Saturday. As with his father before him, you never discussed things with Daddy, he just told you what was what and that was that. There was never any question that it would be done and we certainly never thought about talking back to him. The most that we could muster in protest was to roll our eyes and that action had better not be too obvious—that is, he'd better not see us do it.

Of course, as soon as Daddy left the room, Jimmy said, "I am not going! There's no way I am going to pick berries in the summer heat and get chiggers!" and Patricia said, "Me neither! I'm not going either." So for the rest of the evening they voiced their protests, but they were careful that Daddy did not overhear.

At six o'clock the next morning, Daddy came into the room and said, "Get up and get ready." By the time I looked out the kitchen window, there was Daddy followed by Jimmy and Patricia, with their pants tucked into their socks, straw hats on their heads, and each carrying a bucket that would hold a peck of berries. Patricia and Jimmy both had newspapers in their buckets. Later I asked them why they had carried the newspapers, and Patricia told me, "In case we have to use the bathroom, silly!" Now that Daddy was safely out of the house, I could not contain my laughter. I split my sides laughing as I thought about those two, determined that they were not going to pick black-berries, now both looking like overgrown "Little Rascals."

Upon their return that night, I had never seen them so tired. They each had tanned deeply from the summer sun. They had little chigger bites all over their hands and faces. Their hands were stained dark blue/purple from the berries. Patricia's only comment was, "It was awful, just awful!"

I could not help but laugh. I quoted them mockingly, "I know I'm not going blackberry picking!" Then I laughed some more. Jimmy didn't say a word. He just took a bath and went to bed.

I seemed to enjoy the pie even more, knowing that Jimmy and Patricia picked the berries. When I had finished, I told Mother that I was spending the night up to Aunt Lillian's, and she reminded me to tell Mr. Wilford that I could not work on Friday, the Fourth of July, because we were going to the mountains for a picnic. I said, "Ike and I are getting up early on Thursday to make sure that we get all of our work done so we can have the Fourth off." I took my bath and headed next door. Ike was already upstairs in bed, reading in the dimly lit room. I climbed into my bed and we started to talk.

Ike wanted to know, "Why does DePapa's house have so many bedrooms?" I reminded Ike that DePapa and Big Momma had had 11 boys and a girl.

Daddy had said that DePapa had purchased this house, which at the time had only four rooms, through a white man. He said, "It was difficult back then for blacks to buy houses or other property," and he told us DePapa had asked a Mr. Mull to purchase the house for him and then he was to repay him over time. "But," he added, "Mr. Mull took advantage of DePapa and demanded that he work for him whenever Mr. Mull wanted him to. Even when DePapa was working for others, Mr. Mull would demand that he stop those jobs and come work for him." DePapa had told Daddy, "Don't ever get a white man to buy your house for you!" Daddy told us that the interesting thing about the relationship with the Mull family is that they liked DePapa. When Mr. Mull died, they sent for DePapa to bath and dress Mr. Mull.

I told Ike that Daddy said the two rooms downstairs and three bedrooms upstairs had been added as the family grew. We had lived with my grandparents until I was three, but by that time everybody had left home except Aunt Lillian. My parents had occupied the middle room downstairs. Big Momma had slept upstairs in her own room until she could no longer climb the steps because of her arthritis, and her room was now a guestroom. The upstairs bedroom facing our house was used for storage so Ike and I slept in the third upstairs bedroom, which faced the Carsons' house. The room was small with twin windows. The ceiling sloped on either side of the windows, following the contour of the roof. There were twin iron beds, a little dresser, and a small closet. In the middle of the room was the "slop jar." Though indoor plumbing had been installed and a bathroom added, anyone sleeping upstairs still used the slop jar rather than make the trip down the flight of stairs in the dark. I certainly had no intention of going anywhere in the dark!

We talked a lot about our experiences during the summer. It had been a good summer so far. We had worked really hard and would get our first pay at the end of the day on Thursday. It was a turning point. We were halfway through the summer.

I asked Ike, "What was the best part of the summer?" and without hesitating, he said, "Riding the horse." Ike loved that horse and loved to pretend that he was in the wild west, riding on the plains, even though he only could ride the horse between Mr. Wilford's house and the barn at the end of the garden. But it seemed that the ride to the barn at the end of the day made all the work we did worthwhile.

I told Ike, "I liked riding the horse, but I sure did enjoy meeting Frances when we went to Bridgewater."

Ike asked me again, "Was that the first time you been French kissed?"

"Heck, no! I've been kissed lotsa times." I didn't dare admit that it definitely had been the first time I was French-kissed.

"You know Ike, when I went to bed that evening, I kept thinking about Frances. In fact, I dreamed about her that night. I dreamed that we were French-kissing and holding each other tight and rubbing against each other."

"What happened in the dream?"

"Nothing, but when I woke up, my pajama bottoms were wet in front."

Ike laughed. "You had a wet dream! It means that you are not getting enough. I never have wet dreams now that I have a steady girlfriend in Durham."

"Look at this package of rubbers," Ike said as he pulled a small package from his pants pocket. "Everybody ought to carry rubbers. You never know when you might need one and you definitely don't want to get some girl pregnant." He opened one and showed me, "That's a rubber. You use these to keep a girl from getting pregnant."

Oh, "I keep some rubbers in my drawer at home just in case," I said, knowing that I did not even know how to get one of those things on. It didn't really matter; at 12 years old and living in Morganton, I doubted that I would have a use for one anytime soon.

Two Dollars

The next morning we were up at 5:30 a.m. DePapa was having coffee while Aunt Lillian cooked some grits and fried bacon. We finished eating and were in the Carsons' yard by 6:00 a.m. While we were waiting for Mr. Wilford to come out of the house, I noticed for the first time that summer, how beautiful the morning glories were. Shaped like the end of a trumpet, the deep dark purple of the rim of the horn slowly faded into a pale blue toward the center of the flower. Yet as beautiful as the morning glory was, it was not a flower, but a "weed." It was a constant chore to dig them up by at the roots; otherwise they would spread over the entire garden. I suppose that this was the reason I had never before thought of the morning glory as a beautiful flower.

Mr. Wilford came out of the house without saying a word and headed down to his basement where he gathered two large shovels. He gave one to each of us and said that it was time to fertilize the tomato plants for the last time this year. We got into the truck and drove down to the barn. He backed up right in front of the small corral that surrounded the front of the barn. He told me to shovel all of the manure mixed with straw onto the bed of the truck. All during the year, he usually collected the manure from the barn and the corral and made a pile until the manure ripened. Several times a year, this ripened manure could be used without burning the plants.

Mr. Wilford had four gardens, but grew tomatoes only in the garden on the side of his house and on the side of his father's, Reverend Carson's, house. All morning he would drop a half shovel full of manure along side of the tomato plants and it was our job to work the manure into the soil. We had to be very careful that the manure did not come into contact with the plant. The manure had seasoned, but still could burn the plants if not mixed properly into the soil. It was still smoking when we loaded it onto the truck.

After we had fertilized all of the tomatoes, Mr. Wilford told us to wash the manure residue from the truck bed and then give the dogs some fresh water. This was an unusually hot day and he wanted to be sure that the dogs did not dehydrate.

While we watered the dogs, Ike pointed out, "There is something wrong with the goat! It is lying on its side and will not get up!" Repeating Ike's words verbatim, I ran and told Mr. Wilford who was across the street, "There is something wrong with the goat! It's lying on its side and will not get up!"

Mr. Wilford said, "It's time for the goat to have its kid."

We walked back across the street and into his back yard. By the time we got there, you could see the head of the kid coming out. While we had rabbits and dogs, this was the first time that I'd ever seen anything being born. As the nanny goat lay on her side, the baby's head fully emerged and then the neck. The nanny goat stood up and moved about in an attempt to help the kid come out. Finally, the front legs hit the ground just before the kid fully emerged.

Mr. Wilford said, "The little Billy goat will be fine. Leave it alone with its mother. She'll clean up the kid and start nursing it."

"We'll see you after lunch," Ike said to Mr. Wilford. Mr. Wilford walked up the back steps into the kitchen without replying.

On the way home, Ike said, "Did you know, Johnny, that a baby is born the same way, except the mother goes into the hospital where she sits on a table with her feet spread apart and resting on two posts?"

"How do you know that?"

"I just know. City kids always know more than country kids."

Since I considered myself to live neither in the city nor in the country, I seemed to know less than most people. That day, Ike ate lunch at my house, where Mother had already prepared some tomato sandwiches. She had used a huge ripened tomato and placed one slice on bread that had been spread with salad dressing. A little salt and lots of pepper completed the sandwich. I asked for an onion sandwich with salad dressing, salt and pepper. The onion, too, had come out of the garden and was large, white, and sweet.

We finished eating and got ready to go back to work. "Don't work too late because we have to get ready for the picnic tomorrow," Mother said as we were leaving. I thought to myself, "Hmph. What does it take to prepare for a picnic?"

Our afternoon assignments included washing down the floor of the stable and putting new hay on the floor and in the corral; cleaning the plow, shovel, and other garden instruments; cleaning out the little house in back of Reverend Carson's yard; collecting the slop from the kitchen at the State hospital, feeding and watering the horse, hogs, dogs, and goats; and sweeping the front porches and side walks and hosing them down. It was nearly 7:00 p.m. and Mother had said "Don't work too late!" Mr. Wilford came out as we were putting the hose away. Without saying a word, he gave each of us our summer pay—two dollars apiece! Boy, were we disappointed!

When I got home, I complained to Mother, "I was going to buy a pair of Bermuda shorts to wear on the picnic, but the money I got from Mr. Wilford isn't enough to buy 'em!" Mother said she would see what she could do to help.

CHAPTER V:
THE PICNIC

Mother and Daddy were up before daybreak. Mother had already made the custard for the ice cream and it was cooling on the cabinet. She was also cooking green beans with ham hocks. The potato salad had been made the night before and was in the refrigerator. Daddy was in the yard cleaning his 1951 Plymouth inside and out. I couldn't ever remember him cleaning out the trunk or even polishing the car before.

When I woke up, I found a pair of khaki shorts on the chair in my room. I put them on and found my favorite black and white striped knit shirt. With my long black socks and loafers, I was ready for the picnic. It was only later when I was searching for my khaki long pants that I realized that Mother had cut off my pants to make me my wished-for pair of Bermuda shorts.

After I finished dressing, I walked around the house to where Daddy was working on the car. He told me, "Come with me to town." We went down to the ice plant and selected two large blocks of ice and had them ground into small chunks and bagged. Daddy, in an unusually talkative mood, told me, "When I was little, we used to cut ice from the pond in the winter and store it in our ice house. The icehouse was partially below the ground. We would pack the ice house with blocks of ice and cover them with straw. The ice would usually last into summer." If Daddy was in the right mood, sometimes he would go on and on about growing up in Morganton in the 1920s.

He said, "Momma canned fruit and vegetables all summer. Today families can buy their canned goods at the supermarket; but we had to can anything we wanted after the growing season was over. My Momma even made barrels of sauerkraut from the cabbages we grew. We raised hogs during the year and killed them in the fall. While we ate some fresh meat, we would also rub salt and pepper into the hams and hang them in the smoke house to cure."

"Did you ever eat any 'possum?" Daddy asked.

"I ate some of the 'possum that old man Avery brought to DePapa. I remember that Aunt Lillian baked it with a sweet potato in its mouth," I said.

By the time we reached home, Daddy had talked about how his grandfather loved 'possum and could catch one with his bare hands. "Johnny, you know my uncle Felix would eat anything that moved—rabbits, 'possum, squirrel, raccoon, and of course anything he could catch with a line and pole, including turtle. I think back in those days, they had to eat what they could get."

As we carried the crushed ice across the back yard, I thought, "I'm glad we get most of our food from the store!"

We brought the ice into the house, where mother had already prepared the ice cream churn. She had filled the central metal container with the custard until it was over two-thirds full. She placed the lid on and secured the slightly rusted metal turner into place. She filled the ice cream maker with ice, occasionally adding salt. Jimmy and I took turns churning the ice cream. It took about 20 minutes of turning the handle until the custard was frozen.

Then Mother removed the top and pulled out the dasher. After scraping most of the ice cream from the dasher with a large spoon, she gave the dasher to us to lick the rest of the ice cream that was clinging to its sides. She made a homemade stopper for the lid out of a Wonder Bread wrapper and filled the top of the churn with ice and salt. She placed several sections of the newspaper over the top and secured them to slow the rate of the ice melting.

Ike pestered me about the picnic, "When are we leaving? Who all is going? Where are we going? What are we going to eat?"

"The only thing I know is that we're leaving this morning for the mountains and we'll meet everybody else down by the church. Now you know as much as I do." I thought that parents go to great lengths to keep their children in the dark. Information from adults to kids in the 50s was on a "need to know" only basis.

As the departure time approached, we learned that Jimmy, David, Tommy, Ike and I would ride with Mr. Gaither. Patricia would have to ride with Mother, Daddy, Aunt Lillian, and DePapa. We drove to the back of Slades Chapel, where we met our cousin Oliver, his wife Izola, and daughter Jean. Wilhelmina Page, whom I secretly liked, came with her father, the minister of Gaston Chapel, and his wife. Elbert Crisp, another cousin, was joined by his wife and sister. Boonie Fleming, Bessie his wife, his daughter Sweetcake, and son Frank were in another car. They were followed by Edward McGimpsey, Carl Evans, Harvey Brewer, Gilbert McGalliad, and Forney Happoldt and their families.

Besides being the local barber, Elbert Crisp along with his brother Willie Crisp, Edward McGimpsey, and our cousin, Oliver Fleming, were also the local business entrepreneurs. Together, these men started Ebony Enterprises, which included the first and only funeral home for Negroes in Morganton. In the 50s, the white Kirksey and Soussoman's Funeral Homes would take black people's bodies and embalm them, but would not allow Negroes to have wakes or funerals on their premises. Families had to take the bodies home until it was time for the burial.

The Ebony Funeral Home was started in a building near Slades Chapel AME church. It was located in a wood framed building that had been painted, but no one could remember just when. The Home had a front room for greeting visitors and a middle room where bodies could be viewed. There were naked light bulbs hanging from the ceiling, providing just enough light to be able to identify your next of kin. It was important to Negro families that their deceased family member look like him or herself when they were laid out for the viewing. White funeral homes could never quite get a black person's makeup right. A person never said of white-funeral-home-embalmed bodies that "they looked so natural." Thanks to the Crisp brothers, Oliver Fleming, and Edward McGimpsey, it was reassuring for Negro families to know, during their time of grief, that they did not have to go through the humiliation of being treated as second-class citizens plus having their loved one's face poorly made-up.

My first encounter with a dead body was when my grandmother, Big Momma, died. I had just turned four years old when she died, so I don't remember a lot about her. I can't remember ever seeing her walk. My first memory is of her is in bed in the middle bedroom of the house. She had had her leg amputated because of "a bad case of sugar." Later, the first thing I did every morning after we moved from DePapa's house, was to go up to Aunt Lillian's. I would march dutifully past Big Momma's room and say, "Good morning, Big Momma." Once I had greeted Big Momma, I was free to go into the kitchen to see what Aunt Lillian was doing.

Big Momma died shortly after we moved into our new cinder block house next door. All of her sons came home for the funeral. The white funeral home took Big Momma's body to be embalmed. The next day, she was returned in this beautiful casket. She was placed in the living room right in front of the double windows, which faced Concord Street. The living room had a large black cast-iron stove that was connected to the bricked up fireplace by a stovepipe. There were two easy chairs and a matching sofa and a well-worn Persian rug on the floor. The piano was placed against the wall nearest the dining room. On another wall was an old picture of "the potato digger." On the wall leading to the hallway was the recent picture of DePapa and Big Momma, taken with their children and grandchildren at their 50th wedding anniversary. There I sat on the left arm of my grandfather, the youngest of the grandchildren.

I was too little to see Big Momma in the casket. When Uncle John came home, I asked him to lift me up so I could see my grandmother. Everyone said that she looked so peaceful, while I thought that she looked just like Big Momma. The family had come together as one and had accepted Big Momma's death as the natural end to life. I was not afraid, not even when I saw my Daddy cry. He didn't exactly cry – a tear slowly rolled down his cheek when he learned that his mother had died. At four years old, I was too young to feel any strong emotions because I did not know the meaning of death. Big Momma, I was told, was "gone to heaven," but I could still see her lying in the casket.

Most everyone in town was pleased that Oliver Fleming and his business partners had started the Ebony Funeral Home. Of course, there were a few people who still preferred to be treated as second-class citizens and kept sending the bodies of their relatives to white people for burial. But we were proud of our cousin. Oliver had been a school principal and was highly educated. I heard that he had a "master's degree," which must have meant something to the white school board.

Oliver and his wife, Izola, had gone to Shaw University in Raleigh, where they met as undergraduates. Izola was very light-skinned and came from Ahoskie. Ahoskie was a community in eastern North Carolina, where most of the Negroes were very light-skinned and looked nearly white. These "black" people were very proud of their color and married among themselves in order to keep their light skin and "good hair" in the family. Oliver used to say in front of his wife that her relatives wanted to know where she found a man who was so black. While Oliver took the jokes and teasing in stride, Ahoskie had a reputation for not welcoming blacks who were considered too dark. Izola was very different from her family and neighbors in Ahoskie. Izola had an attitude much like my grandmother Margaret who, though she could easily pass for white, did not see color. Oliver was black in complexion, much darker than either of his parents. Oliver's father, Noah, and my grandfather, DePapa, were brothers, so Oliver and my father, James, were first cousins.

Oliver gave up his job as principal in order to start the Ebony Funeral Home. He later branched out and opened the Ebony Grill. It was the first time I knew what the word "Ebony" meant. Black people were proud of their color, but preferred not to be "too black." They were also proud of the progress of the race, and the opening of Ebony Funeral Home, Ebony Grill, and the Ebony Pool Room signaled progress for the race, not just for Oliver. It was significant that they chose the name "Ebony" for their businesses. So when a white man once came into the barbershop and asked directions to the "E-bone-nee" Grill, Elbert proudly informed him of the correct pronunciation.

Daddy would take us to the Ebony Grill for ice cream Sundaes and banana splits. It was a great feeling to be able to walk into a café and not have to worry about being asked to leave because they did not serve coloreds.

Besides being a partner in Ebony Enterprises, Elbert Crisp also owned Crisp's Barber Shop and was related to my grandmother by way of my great great grandmother whose name was Mona Crisp. Mona was a free person of color who attended the white Presbyterian Church. Mona lived just like a white woman. Tradition had it that she never wore shoes in summer or winter. I never knew just how Elbert came to be our cousin, I just accepted the fact.

Gaston Chapel and Slades Chapel Churches anchored the black business district of Morganton. Each church had an adjacent parsonage, all located on East Union Street, which dissected the town from east to west. Moving east on Union Street you passed Slades Chapel, the parsonage, the funeral home, the poolroom, Ebony Grill, and the barbershop on the right side of the street.

Daddy had strict rules regarding what we could and could not do. We had to attend church and could go as many times as we liked; no restrictions there. We had to get our hair cut at the barbershop, but we could not linger. We could go to the Ebony Grill if we had any money, but we could not go into the poolroom under any circumstances. Those were the rules. We knew them and everybody else in town knew them. Violate these rules or any of his other rules and he found out through his network of what appeared to us to be spies, we were in deep trouble. Daddy did not tolerate breaking the rules.

So we all met in the Negro business district to start our picnic. The men who were elders and leaders in the church had organized the picnic as thoroughly as if it were a cross-country caravan. Elbert Crisp drove the lead car, and Oliver drove the car that served as the "caboose." Willie Crisp, the picnic organizer, then determined the order of the cars between the lead car and the caboose. Willie Crisp acted like a born leader. He was always dressed to a "T." People said he had his own orchestra before moving back to Morganton. Anyway, we found ourselves somewhere around the middle of the picnic caravan.

It seemed like it was already afternoon by the time we got started around 10:00 a.m. The caravan drove out of town on Greene Street, which then became State Route (SR) 181, which went from the piedmont up to the mountains. As we gradually ascended toward Grandfather Mountain, the road meandered back and forth, all the while steadily gaining in altitude. The adult men had planned the trip with all the precision of a military exercise. The adult women probably had access to more information than what was shared with the children, but we knew very little when we started out and learned where we were going as we proceeded.

The plan was to travel along Skyline Drive and take detours to such places as Linville Caverns, Blowing Rock, Grandfather Mountain, and Table Rock. By the time we reached the mountains through slowly snaking our way up the steep and curvy roads, the weather had changed from a sunny day, to a gray, overcast day. But nothing dampened the spirits of our group. The Smoky Mountains were a sight to behold and were named for the misty, low-lying clouds that formed, re-formed and clung to the mountains. The cool damp air had little effect on the spirits of the party. There were few public places that Negroes could take their families without facing discrimination, and the state and national park systems provided two of those places.

We traveled first to Linville Cavern. I never liked going too far underground and was careful to keep an eye on the ceiling of the cavern in case it started to collapse. The caverns maintained a constant year-round temperature. The stalactites and stalagmites made all sorts of unusual and interesting formations. We saw what appeared to be a pipe organ and a human face, and we observed a pond filled with blind fish that lived in constant darkness. While we saw Table Rock only from a distance, we went right up to both Blowing Rock and Chimney Rock. I was fascinated by the updraft in what looked like a chimney. Objects dropped over the chimney would float down and then be blown upwards again. Blowing Rock provided a vista unsurpassed east of the Mississippi River. The blue-green mountains, dusted by the smoky mist, were beautiful even to a 12-year old boy. I could understand why rich white people in Morganton purchased summer homes in Blowing Rock. What I did not understand was why teachers like Esther and Lucille Carson served as housekeepers and cooks for these families during the summer.

By three o'clock you could hear rumblings among the adults about how hungry they were. The smaller kids had been hungry since noon, while the rest of us did not start complaining until around 1:00 p.m. Our leaders finally found the place where we were to have our feast. As was tradition in the South, the men and boys carried the food from the cars and the women prepared the food and set the table. And what a table it was! There were homemade rolls, potato salad enriched with real Hellmann's mayonnaise and dozens of deviled eggs, baked beans full of molasses and smoked bacon, macaroni and creamy cheddar cheese, collard greens and ham hocks, three bean salad, green beans and ham (that Mother had prepared along with potato salad), a country ham, and mounds and mounds of golden fried chicken.

There was a completely separate dessert table. There was a pound cake so rich with butter it saturated the paper towel on which it sat, a coconut cake with double-boiler icing and real coconut, a carrot cake, a double chocolate cake, a pecan pie, an apple pie, and a peach cobbler. We topped off all this with our homemade ice cream.

We ate and ate overloaded plates of food. It was a Thanksgiving feast in midsummer. There was plenty to drink, too—Pepsi, Coca Cola, the new Lotta Cola, ginger ale, and Orange Crush (my favorite). Some of the ladies had made sweetened ice tea and ice cold lemonade. There was a special place over to the side where the men would go, pull a can from the cooler, and place the can into a paper bag. I saw a few men near Boonie's car, pouring what looked like water from a canning jar into paper cups. We all knew that it was special "white lightning" liquor purchased from a local bootlegger.

I was getting ready to tell Ike about my experience with white lightning when he said, "I bet you never had so much as a drink of beer, Johnny."

"I have too. I had some white lightning! I bet you never had any white lightning!"

"I don't believe you, Johnny. You never had any white lightning."

"I did so. It was on one of our vacations to Jacksonville to visit my Aunt Em. I must have been about five or six years old. My Aunt Em loved to entertain. She gave great parties with lots of good food, especially seafood. As a boy of five, I kept wondering why the men and some of the women kept going into the kitchen and pouring little glasses of water out of a Mason jar. So, when no one was looking, I pulled a chair up to the counter and poured me a little glass of that water out of the Mason jar. I drank it quickly. A terrible burning sensation hit me as soon as the liquor passed down my throat. I quickly started drinking regular water directly from the tap! Fearing that someone would find out what I had done, I went out to play with the neighborhood kids, slightly high on white lightning."

Ike said, "I was ten before I took a drink. I did not much like it. I prefer beer."

Then I told Ike about the time we had found gallons of white lightning in the cemetery. "Jimmy, Tommy, and I were roaming around the cemetery the way we usually did when we came upon our cousin Charles, crawling on his hands and knees as if he was looking for something. When he saw us, he did not get up. 'What's wrong?' we asked him.

'Go on home,' Charles said. Well, Charles wasn't old enough to tell us what to do. We didn't have to obey him, so we continued roaming around the cemetery when some white policemen came up to us. They were looking for bootleg whisky and wanted to know if we knew of any stills in the area. Of course we didn't and probably would not have told them if we had. But anyway, the next thing we knew there was Charles walking down the cemetery road with the two police officers. They had evidently seen Charles on the ground with several quarts of white lightning under his coat. We had no idea that Charles was trying to sneak away with the booze he had found! The next day, there was an article in the paper about three boys playing cowboys and Indians, who found illegal whiskey in the cemetery. We were mad 'cause we were not playing cowboys and Indians. That was what little kids did! We were glad that the paper did not list our names."

After Ike and I finished eating our picnic lunch, we watched the men play cards. The men liked to gossip just like the women, but they called it "talking men's business."

I heard Elbert ask Oliver, "What's going on in your neighborhood?"

"What do you mean?" Oliver replied.

"I hear that you have had some break-ins on Concord Street. Anything important get stolen?"

"I haven't heard a thing. Neither Izola or any of my sisters mentioned anything about a theft."

Looking at me, Oliver asked, "Have you heard anything about thefts in the neighborhood, Johnny?"

"Will said something a week ago about somebody missing a pie. I think it might have been Miss Mae Lee, but she maybe just thought she made a pie. At least that's what I heard Miss Lucille say."

The women talked in several groups, but I could not hear what they were saying. The kids played all sorts of games, including horseshoes, badminton, and volleyball. The preteens walked along the trails, some holding hands, but only after getting out of sight of their parents. Jimmy was talking to a girl and I wanted to talk to Wilhelmina. We had talked outside of Linville Caverns. Wilhelmina was such a pretty name. She was light-skinned with long black hair. Her hair never seemed to be "fixed"—it just flowed from her head to her shoulders and midway down her back. She had a wonderful smile. I know that she liked me, at least as a friend. I saw her later with Frank Fleming, Boonie's son, who was nearly 14.

Ike and I just sat on the side of the cliff and fed the squirrels, which had become tame. With so much human contact, they would actually eat out of your hands. I decided to take this opportunity to ask Ike about the trouble he had been in last year in Durham.

"You got in trouble during the school year in Durham, didn't you? That's why your daddy sent you to Morganton, right?"

Ike started to talk as if he was relieved at having the opportunity to tell his side of what happened, "I got mixed up with a group of older boys. They were like a gang and would take money from the younger kids. I guess it was pretty easy for them to go from taking money from little kids to robbing old people. I never robbed anyone, but I was associated with the group that did. When they were caught, we were all arrested, and several old people came forward to testify against us. Nearly all of us were sentenced to reform school."

I asked, "Why didn't you go to reform school, too?"

He said, "My daddy asked Uncle John to write what they called a "character letter" and had him take it to the prosecuting attorney. You know our uncle is a minister, Johnny, and he's very high up in the State Baptist Convention. He also works at Shaw University. So he has a reputation even in the white community. He promised that he would see that I did not get in trouble and that I would behave in the future. He told the judge about his father in Morganton and that Louie would arrange for me to spend the summer in Morganton living with their father. They talked to Wilford about hiring me and thought it would be a good idea for both of us to work together for the summer. I suppose since you have always talked about being a minister, they thought that some of your good behavior would rub off on me."

Ike made me think about why I wanted to be a minister. I was definitely afraid of going to Hell. Hell was real for me, maybe more real than Heaven. I didn't know whether I wanted to be a minister out of fear of going to Hell as opposed to any real desire to serve God. But whatever the motivation behind my commitment, I had decided to make a real sacrifice and become a missionary. I believed that service as a missionary would keep me from burning eternally in Hell because I had a real vision of what Hell was like. Reverend Moore, the white Pentecostal preacher, often visited DePapa and showed slides of sinners burning in hell. He gave very vivid descriptions of what fire and brimstone were like and what it was like to burn forever and not be consumed by the fire.

So I am not so sure that there was such a big difference between Ike and me. Would I have been more like Ike had good church people not frightened me to death? Would Ike have been more like me if someone had scared him into being good?

As we continued to talk, I asked, "What do you plan to do with your life?"

He said, "I want to go to college, but I don't know what I want to study, since I don't like school. I promised God that I would change when I became an adult, but for now I have to be who I am, trouble or not."

Ike's revelation took me by surprise. It had never occurred to me that one could make an agreement to be bad for a period of time and then decide to be good. And what did being "bad" mean? I had never thought that there was much difference in behavior between Ike and me. Yes, Ike would curse on occasion. He said that he had had sex, but I did not believe him. He fought sometimes and I didn't like to fight. I really had to be pushed hard to fight.

"Ike, do you believe that something can come true if you dream it?"

"Huh? What are you talking about?" he asked.

"You know, if you have a dream and then you act out that dream. What I mean is, last year I had this dream about this boy named Robert Jenkins, who had been bullying the kids in the fourth grade. Robert had failed the fifth grade and was kept back. That's how he got into my class. He was a small kid with red hair. He had a brother in high school who was a nice guy. But Robert always seemed to have something to prove. He had to have his way, no matter what. Maybe it was because he was so short. And most of the time he did get his way. People, including me, would just give in.

Well, one night I dreamed that I stood up to Robert Jenkins. I dreamed that I told him off and he backed down. It's funny the way things happen; but the very next day, we were playing ball for real when Robert decided that he wanted to play first baseman. Since I was the first baseman, he came up to me and told me that he was taking over and for me to leave the field. When he said that I remembered my dream and it took on a life of its own. Well, I got right up in Robert Jenkins' face and told him that I wasn't leaving and that I wanted to know what he was going to do about it. He hesitated for a moment and then just walked off the field. From that day forward, I never had any more trouble out of Robert Jenkins."

"Yeah, I think something like that can happen. You already believe that you can whip this guy, so you have the self confidence to do it," Ike said.

"I think you are right."

While I did not say this to Ike, I thought that he was basically a good kid. I think that the gang members in Durham influenced him. Uncle Louie had made a good choice in sending him to Morganton. I looked at Ike as if I were seeing him for the first time. Of all Uncle Louie's children, Ike resembled both his parents, Alice and Louie, the most. He had his mother's eyes and nose, but definitely had the Fleming head—big with a hairline that grew low on the forehead. He had my uncle Louie's smile. Ike had great, almost perfect, white teeth and when he grinned, he showed nearly all them with the widest smile of any person I knew. Ike was taller than I was and still very thin. For a city boy, he could work as hard as any man. I looked at Ike and he looked at me. We agreed, "That's enough talk, let's go and get some more dessert!"

It did not rain that day, but it was cloudy and misty all afternoon and into the evening. The women began putting on their sweaters. The men, now a little heavier from all the food they had eaten, started to load the cars with bundles, baskets, and coolers that were much lighter than they were a few hours earlier. The desserts were the last thing to pack, what few that were left. Ike and I both had another piece of blackberry pie and a piece of pound cake. At 12 years old and nearly 5'8", I still weighed only 125 pounds and could eat anything I wanted.

Elbert, Oliver, Daddy, and several other men decided that it was time to go. I never knew how the men reached these decisions, but it seemed that everybody else was ready to go, too. The drive home was slow and uneventful. We traveled back with Mr. Gaither. It was nighttime when we reached Morganton. We were all ready to turn in after a long and wonderful summer day.

Will was up to Aunt Lillian's, waiting for us to get back. When Will waited hours for someone to return, it meant that he had some news he wanted to tell—some important news.

Will said, "Where's Toots? I need to talk to Toots."

Aunt Lillian said, "He's on his way, now."

When Daddy drove up into the yard, Will immediately went over to the car and said, "Toots, I got to talk to you. It's important."

Daddy said, "What's the problem, Will?" Ike and I leaned against the tree in the front yard so we could hear.

"While you were away, there were a series of break-ins. I am sure it is the work of the 'goatman' who is now camped out near Broughton Hospital," Will said.

Daddy and Will continued to talk. Ike said, "Johnny, what do you think is going on?"

"I don't know. I heard Mr. Crisp talking to Oliver earlier today about some thefts, but I don't know what's going on. But right now, I'm tired and I want to go to bed." We knew that we would explore this further, but not that night.

CHAPTER VI:
SUNDAYS

Sunday was not a typical day of the week in our house and community because a boy certainly could not sleep late. We were up by 8:00. Mother made pancakes, our favorite breakfast. She used a large black cast iron skillet into which she would drop three equal amounts of batter to make three perfectly round pancakes. Servings always came in threes. You either ate three, six, or nine pancakes. Seldom did any one eat 12. I generally ate nine with four pieces of bacon. Mother would cut the bacon in half to fit into her smaller cast iron frying pan. For us, a whole piece of bacon counted as two. We smothered our pancakes in Log Cabin syrup with lots of butter. Once a week, Daddy and Mr. Wilford drove out to the country to purchase fresh butter, eggs, and buttermilk from Miss Poole. Miss Poole was related to my Mother, but we still called her "Miss Poole." She raised enough dairy cattle and chickens to sell milk, butter, and eggs to relatives, friends, and local families. Her butter greatly enriched our Sunday morning breakfasts.

Our routine on Sundays was to eat, read the paper, get properly dressed and go to Sunday School at Slades Chapel AME Zion Church. DePapa was an elder and when he was younger, had often walked to Church before anybody else was ready. Mother went to St. Stephen's Episcopal Church on Bouchelle Street. Bouchelle Street extended from town through several white neighborhoods and into the black neighborhood. The interesting thing about black and white neighborhoods in Morganton was that there was no clear line of demarcation. One led naturally into the other. Yet, the symbolic boundaries were as clear as a bright red line down the street. There was virtually no social contact between the two races. St. Stephen's Church was an anomaly in what was otherwise a strict code of social contact. St. Sephens had a white priest, the bishop was white, and often "liberal" whites from Morganton and surrounding communities would visit the church, especially when the Episcopal bishop came.

The church was initially located behind Grace Church, the white Episcopal Church. A new Negro Episcopal church was built on Bouchelle Street in the 1940s. I suppose it was considered more appropriate to have a Negro church in a Negro neighborhood. The Avery family donated the land. Miss Annie Avery was the church organist and her brother, Father Eugene Avery, was the only Negro Episcopal priest I ever knew until I left North Carolina. Father Avery married my Daddy's first cousin, Elizabeth Fleming.

The church was located on Bouchelle Street right on the dividing line between the white and black neighborhoods. At the end of the street were the BFW club and the colored recreation center. We had to walk down Bouchelle to get to the recreation center; while we could walk to the recreation Center, Daddy strictly prohibited us from going anywhere else. I think he believed half of the rumors he heard about what went on in and around Bouchelle Street. While there were many prominent families who lived on the street, the farther down one went on Bouchelle, the more of a reputation the street had for unsavory activities. We generally did not go to St. Stephen's because it did not have a Sunday school, but that would change within the year. But for now, we attended Sunday School at Slades Chapel.

During the spring and summer, we walked to Sunday School unless it rained. Sunday School started promptly at 9:30 a.m. There were various classes, depending on your age group. I was in the intermediate class. We met upstairs in the Church sanctuary. The senior class also met in the sanctuary. I always thought it was funny that DePapa and other church people his age would be in Sunday school, but DePapa said, "You're never too old to learn!" and he knew his Bible backward and forward.

Daddy drove to church that morning with his sister, Aunt Lillian, and gave rides to anyone else he saw on the way who needed a lift. As we were getting older, Daddy and DePapa expected us to stay for church services. There was not much time between Sunday School and Church. The elders, deacons, and deaconesses would be among the first to arrive, if they were not already at Sunday School. The women ushers wore starched white dresses with white gloves and shoes. The male ushers wore black shoes, dark suits, white shirts, and black ties and white gloves.

This was the Sunday for the Senior Choir to sing. They were in back putting on their dark purple robes. The minister had not yet come in from the parsonage next door. Reverend Duncan was putting the last touches on his sermon. He had it worked out in his head and generally only carried a few small notes with him to the podium. This week the church brochure said that the sermon would be about the Prodigal Son, the parable about two brothers—one who stayed with his father and worked diligently over the years, and the other who asked that his father give him his inheritance which he then proceeded to waste and yet, was forgiven by his father.

Officially, Church started at 11:00 a.m. sharp, but people had their own times of arrival. Some wanted to miss all of the "preliminaries" and were deliberately late. Others were late because they were always late. Miss Lolli Crisp, who had only one arm, was always in church on time. Mrs. Carolyn Crisp was just late enough to make a grand entrance with high heels, a flowing black dress with a ruffled white blouse, and a large brimmed black hat with white piping around the edge of the brim. Everyone came to church dressed in their best finery. All the men wore suits or sports coats and slacks. They all wore ties (even if some could not tie the knot themselves). All the women wore hats. Cousin Delth had the most extraordinary and elaborate hats imaginable. She favored feathered hats and wore hats made from pheasant tail feathers to hats sporting large white flowery ostrich feathers. Many of the women had little black veils attached to their hats. The school-teachers wore very tasteful suits, usually blue or black, but sometimes tweed. Blouses were almost always cream in color. And all the women came to church in high heels. Of course, later, many complained about their feet hurting from wearing shoes that were sometimes a half-size too small.

This Sunday in July was typically hot. All the windows were open and several fans were circulating the hot sticky air. Neither the heat nor cold ever changed the way people dressed for church. They wore their very best because, for many of these working people, church was the only place where they could "look good." Most of the congregation was composed of working class folks. The upper class, if can it can be said that Morganton had an Upper Class Colored Society, was composed of teachers, the funeral home director, the barber, and several store-keepers. There were some mechanics and furniture workers in this category, if these workers had married teachers or nurses. We had no professional Negro lawyers or doctors. Most of the congregation would have been considered middle class in beliefs and practices, though not in economic standing.

The Flemings were middle class, even though my father worked for Drexel Furniture Factory and my mother was a dietician. My grandfather was a brick mason and made a very good living for his family. My mother's mother was white in complexion and had married a barber who had served the white community exclusively. They did not attend Slades Chapel, but were members of St. Stephen's Episcopal Church (hence my mother's attendance there). Most of the founding fathers of St. Stephen's were descendants of Free People of Color. Being white in complexion and descendants of Free People of Color provided standing in both the colored and white communities. I was always amazed at how much respect dark-skinned black folk gave to light-skinned black folk.

The riffraff (as Miss Daisy Avery of St. Stephen's called them) seldom came to church. But there were also individuals who tried to rise above their families' poor reputations and live decent lives. Those who were successful were allowed to come to church and to assume an air of respectability as long as they behaved. Of course, there was always some back-sliding. If this occurred, and they confessed their sins publicly and asked for forgiveness, they were usually allowed back into the body of the church. People from good standing families seldom had to go through this public humiliation. There was certainly a double standard. Many black ministers took an unchristian interest in certain women of the church, but there were seldom any repercussions for the minister. As we sat in church, I leaned over and gave Ike the lowdown.

"Reverend Bullock, the former minister, liked the ladies too much for comfort. They said he pursued anything in a skirt. I once overheard Miss Lucille tell Mother, 'Why, I had to stand in front of that table to keep the Reverend Bullock from trying to look under the table's skirt!' and then they both chuckled.

"But Reverend Bullock made a big mistake when he got interested in Mike Chambers' daughter. Mr. Chambers was very strict with his children, especially his daughters. When they were juniors and seniors in high school, they just blossomed. They were much more mature for their age than the other girls, and had very shapely figures. Whenever Sandra Chambers walked up to the front of the church to place her money in the collections plate, Reverend Bullock's eyes followed her every move."

Ike interrupted, "Yeah, I remember Sandra. She wore some very tight sweaters."

I nodded. "Yeah, she's the one. After Sandra graduated from high school, she enrolled at Johnson C. Smith in Charlotte. Reverend Bullock made several trips to Charlotte to visit Sandra before Mr. Chambers knew anything about it. But then one Saturday afternoon while Mr. Chambers was in the barbershop, Robert White just happened to mention seeing Reverend Bullock at Johnson C. Smith talking to Sandra. I don't think anyone will ever know if Robert White knew Mr. Chambers was sitting there reading the paper but Mr. Chambers didn't need to hear another word. He flung down his paper, stalked over to the parsonage, hit the door with such force, he nearly broke down the door. Rev. Bullock heard all of the commotion and rushed to open the door. You can imagine his shock when he saw the anger in Mr. Chambers' eyes. He instinctively tried to close the door, but Mr. Chambers already had his foot between the fame and the door, preventing Rev. Bullock from shutting it. Holding back his desire to strike Rev. Bullock out of "respect," Mr. Chambers told Rev. Bullock to stay away from his daughter. He told him never to set foot on Johnson C. Smith's campus as long as his daughter was enrolled there or he would have to answer to him."

"Wow, what happened after that? Where is the Reverend now?" Ike asked.

"Oh, the Reverend got a transfer out of this conference and moved to..."

"Johnny, stop talking so much in church," Daddy said, trying to whisper while interrupting my conversation. I had been so involved in telling Ike about Reverend Bullock that I hadn't even seen Daddy come into the church!

Because I was nearly 12, I was not only expected to stay for church, but also to "behave," even if I wanted to do otherwise. I could not get away with some of the things I had done when I was younger, like the time I found a little green rubber snake on the way to Sunday school. Just as with the dead spider I found in the church bathroom and the opportunity that occurred to tease poor Linda Williams with it, without a second thought I automatically picked up the snake and put it in my pocket. I knew that it would come in handy even if I did not know just how. You'd think I would have learned after "the Spider Incident," but I found a use for it that very day. During the church service while the choir was singing "Nearer my God to Thee," I surreptitiously took the snake from my pocket and put it on the shoulder of the lady in front of me. I tapped her shoulder so that she would turn her head toward the snake. When she saw the snake, she screamed, grabbed the snake and threw it across several pews. The snake landed in the lap of another lady, who immediately screamed and did the same thing. Another lady screamed. This was going better than I had hoped! The whole process occurred so systematically throughout the church that the choir thought the congregation was "getting happy" based on their singing. As for me, unfortunately I had made the initial mistake of placing the snake on the shoulder of Miss Margie Fleming, who told my father what I had done. Needless to say, Daddy later gave me a good whipping. So now at my age, most of my mischief took the form of talking during service. Since Daddy had already given me my one and only warning, I decided to be quiet.

That morning, the choir opened the morning worship service with hymn 322, "The Old Rugged Cross." The pianist played the preamble; just before the choir started to sing, they all began to stand as if they had been individually called to rise one at a time. They even started singing the first line of the song consecutively, "On a hill far away..." Not until the words, "stood an old rugged cross," did they finally begin to sing in unity. "...the emblem of suffering and shame, and I loved that old cross for the dearest and best, for the one child of lost sinners, he was slain..." The congregation joined in, "...So I will cherish the old rugged cross till my trophy at last I lay down, so I will cling to that old rugged cross where I found the Lord and where I will change it some day for a crown." This was DePapa's favorite hymn and I can still hear him sing, "I will cherish the old rugged cross and change it one day for a crown." In the AME Church, it did not matter if you couldn't sing. What mattered was that when you sang, you sang with the conviction of your faith.

As the choir ended the last verse, the minister walked up to the pulpit and said, "Good morning, congregation. Blessed be the name of the Lord." He immediately opened the morning worship service with a prayer of thanksgiving. "Dear God, we thank you for this day. We thank you that you allowed us to wake up this morning. We thank you for our mothers and fathers, sisters and brothers, and all of our children. We thank you for our good health and homes. For those of us without homes and jobs, we beseech you to open our hearts that we who are more fortunate will share with those in need." Reverend Duncan asked a special blessing for the Reverend Martin Luther King, Jr., and those working to bring justice into this world. He ended his prayer by asking, "Lord, bless this congregation this morning that we might praise your name. To God be the Glory. Congregation, say 'amen!'" And the congregation responded with a loud "AMEN!"

Then Deacon Avery read the lesson from the New Testament, Luke 15:11-32. "And He said, 'A certain man had two sons. And the younger of them said to his father, 'Father, give me the portion of goods that falleth to me.' And he divided unto them his living.' "

While Deacon Avery read, I wondered just how generous I would be if Jimmy took his share of whatever inheritance we might get and wasted it and then came back for a share of what was left. I thought that I would be angry. Then I heard Deacon Avery say, "And he said unto him, 'Son, thou art ever with me, and all that I have is thine. It is fit that we should make merry and be glad, for this thy brother was dead, and is alive again; and was lost, and is found.'"

Deacon Avery ended the lesson by saying, "Praise be to God."

The congregation recited the Apostle's Creed and the choir sang hymn 456, "Pass me not, oh gentle Savior, hear my humble cry; while on others thou art calling, do not pass me by."

The first collection was the "Missionary Collection." The work of missionaries generally took place in Africa and what with Africa being far away, the Missionary Collection usually generated the least amount of money. Even when the collection plate had been passed halfway through the congregation, you could still hear the jingle of coins dropping into it because so few dollars were placed in the plate that would cushion the sound of the coins. Then, there was the collection for the poor and shut-in, the collection for the presiding elder, and a collection for delegates to attend the state convention. The final collection was the one where members of the congregation were supposed to tithe. Those who did, were allowed to go to the front of the church and place ten percent of their earnings into the plate and walk proudly back to their seats. The ushers then passed the plate for the rest of the congregation to give anonymously.

The money was counted in front of the church and the amount had to be "just right." For example, if the sum came to $107.31, the minister would ask for more donations to bring the total to an even $110. Many Sundays the minister had to ask for more money to get the figure just right. This Sunday the collection came to an astounding $135.00! This was surely encouragement for the pastor to preach a particularly good sermon.

The choir sang, "I go to the garden alone, while the dew is still on the roses..." By the time they sang several verses and returned to the refrain, "...and he walks with me and he talks with me..." the congregation was on the rise. There were a number of ladies already standing and shouting; everyone was swaying with the rhythm of the music and clapping their hands. Herbert Carter began the solo with his deep bass voice, "...and he walks with me..." There were cries of "Sing it!" "Yes, Lord," "Help him, Jesus!" Finally, the choir sang the last refrain and the minister moved into the pulpit.

"Yes, he walks with me and he talks with me and he tells me I am his own..." Reverend Duncan repeated this several times before going back to the New Testament lesson. The Reverend Onslow Duncan had been the minister ever since the untimely departure of Reverend Bullock.

I began to whisper to Ike everything that I knew about Reverend Duncan, while trying not to let Daddy hear me talking again. "I heard that he came from the eastern part of the state. He was educated at Kittrell College, but still preaches the old time way. He is married with three sons, who have graduated and left Morganton for college. Reverend Duncan married a lady named Miss Evelyn Morris from Knoxville, Tennessee. She is very light-skinned. Reverend Duncan shaves his head so it's difficult to tell how much hair he actually has left. His head really shines when he works up a sweat during his sermons."

Reverend Duncan summarized the parable of the prodigal son and turned to his congregation. "How many times has God forgiven us of our sins?" He asked, "Are we not the prodigal son? Have we not squandered our inheritance? Have we not failed to live up to the talents that we have been given? Are we not sinners? Are we not in need of forgiveness? And how many times has God forgiven us our sins?"

The Reverend Duncan slowly worked his congregation up to a fever pitch. He slowly increased the volume of his voice to the point where he was nearly shouting. He was almost ready to "bring the congregation home." Shouts of "Yes, Lord," "Forgive me, Lord," and "Amen!" filled the air.

Miss Corpening was in the aisles, jumping up and down saying over and over, "Jesus, Jesus, Jesus..." Miss Harbison was so overcome that she stood up, threw open her arms, and fell back to the pew. Miss Frankie and Miss Lucille immediately rushed to her side, fanning her, holding her hands, and wiping the sweat from her brow. The congregation was right where Reverend Duncan wanted them to be.

He turned to the congregation and said, "Those of you who are sinners, take this first step. Come down to the altar. Ask God to forgive you of your sins. Who will come down this morning?"

The choir began to sing, "I go to the garden alone, while the dew is still on the roses..." Ike slowly got up. There were tears in his eyes as he walked down the aisle and up to the altar, where he turned to the minister and asked God to forgive him of his sins. Reverend Duncan offered a prayer in Ike's name and asked God to bestow His blessings on this child.

Several more members and non-members of the congregation walked up to Reverend Duncan to seek forgiveness and ask God's blessings. Reverend Duncan called for all of the young people to come to the altar. Raymond Brewer and I walked down the aisle and knelt together. The Minister asked the non-members if they wanted to join the church.

When he came to Raymond Brewer, Raymond said, "I want to join the church across the street." I stifled a laugh and thought, "Then why is he here?"

The choir concluded, "And the joy we share as we tarry there, none other hath ever known," and Reverend Duncan prayed, "Lord, bless these children and give them the strength to do thy will."

As the congregation sat down, the minister concluded, "May the Peace of God, which passes all understanding, keep your heart and soul in the knowledge of God and of his Son Jesus Christ, and may the blessings of God the Father, Son, and Holy Spirit be with you both now and forevermore."

The service ended at 2:08 p.m. as the choir sang, "The Lord be with you 'til we meet again..." Slowly the congregation moved toward the door. Each person spoke to the minister, mostly complimenting him on his sermon. Daddy was already down at the bottom of the steps waiting for DePapa and Aunt Lillian. Several people came up to speak to "Mr. Dee." Aunt Lillian knew everyone and had something to say to each person she knew. Daddy seemed resigned to waiting until she finished several mini-conversations.

Meanwhile, Ike and I decided to walk home. Ike was quiet. He told me, "I was overcome with emotion in church. All I could think about was that I wanted to be good."

Nothing else was said. We quietly walked home.

Sundays never ended with afternoon services. There was always "church" going on somewhere. Aunt Lillian was very ecumenical; she knew no religious boundaries and was just as much at home at Slades Chapel as she was at St. Stephen's Episcopal Church, which she always attended on those occasions when the Episcopal bishop visited the church.

Aunt Lillian was also very comfortable with fundamentalist denominations. She asked Ike and me if we wanted to attend evening services at Green Street Holiness Church. I remembered seeing that church when my brother Jimmy and I went to Boy Scout meetings on Green Street. The church looked like one of those buildings constructed in a flood plain. It was built on stilts with steep wooden stairs in the front. The exterior of the church had been covered with a shingle like material molded into a brick pattern. It did not look like brick, even at a distance. There were no windows in the front of the small one-room church building. On each side, there were three equally-spaced windows. A small steeple adorned the top of the roof.

Ike and I walked all the way to Green Street with Aunt Lillian. It was a typical hot and humid July summer evening. It never occurred to us not to do something just because it was hot and humid. When it was hot, you sweated to cool off. Nobody in our neighborhood had air conditioning. Some of the stores in town like Burand's had air conditioning, but air conditioning made you cold when you were inside and even hotter when you went back outside, where the temperature was in the mid-90s. At home, we had a fan. It was a large black metal fan with large spaces between the frets of the metal frame. It was not a problem for us to get our hands through the metal frame and stop the fan. Sometimes, we allowed the blades of the fan to strike a newspaper to make a noise like a motorcycle engine. Daddy told us not to play with the fan because we might cut our hands, but we "knew what we were doing" and played with it anyway.

Everybody had screens on their windows and doors unless they were really poor. In the summertime, you raised the windows to allow for a breeze to blow through the house to keep it cool. We stayed outside, usually sitting in front of DePapa's house sometimes until late at night. By then, living in the piedmont area of the state, we could expect a cool evening breeze that often became a chilling breeze by morning. On really hot nights, we used the fan, or rather, Mother and Daddy used the fan. Before they built their new bedroom, the fan generally stayed at the corner of the living room where the kitchen and their bedroom intersected. While sitting in the living room, we could all share in the bounty of the fan. At bedtime, the fan was placed in

Mother and Daddy's room. While we may have been hot, we never complained.

We were acclimated to the hot North Carolina summers as we entered the Green Street Holiness Church. Even though services had started by the time we got there, we managed to get very close to the front. This is where the action took place. Sister Katie Vaughn and Brother Randy Collins were on piano this evening. The two most important people to the Holiness congregation were the minister and the piano player, and not necessarily in that order. The minister this evening was Robert C. Franklin. He and Sister Katie were from Forest City. Katie traveled the church circuit with her mother, Reverend Edna Vaughn. Reverend Vaughn had just appeared at Slades Chapel one day unannounced. She was wearing a long black cape over a long black dress. She and her daughter, Katie, always dressed in black. I thought Katie was pretty. She had beautiful dark brown skin like her mother. However, Reverend Vaughn would not let Katie out of her sight. They were inseparable. Katie could not read music. She did what they called "playing by ear." Katie's mother was a self-ordained minister who could always be counted on for a show. Daddy said, "She performs for the Lord."

I liked the Holiness Church. I liked the preaching, stomping, singing, piano playing, and dancing. While I considered myself religious and wanted to be a minister, I felt I could never bring myself to preach and shout the way Reverend Franklin did that night. He whooped and hollered at the top of his voice, accompanied by Randy Collins on the piano. Now, Randy could play. He could move his hands rapidly up and down the keyboard without missing a note. If by chance he did miss a note, we never noticed. By nine o'clock, both he and the minister were sweating profusely. Gladys Tate got up to wipe the sweat from Randy's forehead.

By 9:30, the church was rocking. Every member of the congregation was clapping and stomping their feet. It was only a matter of time before they were dancing in the aisles. Madie Foxx led the way. First she shouted and then danced. Next she danced, then shouted. Finally she shouted while she danced. It was not long before the entire congregation was standing, clapping their hands and moving their feet. Diane Ervin's cousin, Johnny, moved toward the front of the church. Johnny was a tall thin boy of about 17. He was in the back and had gone unnoticed for most of the evening. Johnny said that he wanted to be a minister, which might have explained his reserved, quiet nature. But that night, Johnny "got happy!" I could see his shoulders begin to sway to the music as he approached the front of the church, and when he got to the front of the church, the spirit moved him and he turned around and started dancing in a very spirited way. When the spirit hit them, others joined in danced as if they were possessed by the spirit of the Holy Ghost. Aunt Lillian, Ike and I were moved by the Holy Spirit too; so we were all standing, clapping, singing, dancing, and "getting happy!"

The services continued for another hour before the congregation was completely exhausted. Even though we did not dance as intensely as the members of the church, we had spent our energy and were tired as we prepared ourselves for the long walk home. As we walked in the first cool breeze of the evening, Aunt Lillian told Ike that everybody was very proud that he had decided to give his life to the Lord.

She told Ike, "If your Daddy could have seen you in church this morning, I know he would tell you how proud he is of you. You should take this opportunity to turn your life around, especially once you get back to Durham. Don't be influenced by what others do or say. Be your own man. Don't do anything that will worry your Daddy and your Momma."

Aunt Lillian continued, "You come from strong stock—your people come from Africa! They endured the hardships of crossing the ocean and generations of enslavement right here in Burke County. You and Johnny pass right by the Avery plantation every time you go over to the Deaf School. That's where our people lived and worked as slaves. If they made it through slavery, you can survive and stay out of trouble when you go back to Durham."

We stopped for a moment as Aunt Lillian turned to look us right in the eyes. "You and Johnny have done well all summer. Wilford told Papa that he was proud of how you worked and what a good job you have done. If Wilford said you did a good job, then you did an excellent job," Aunt Lillian said. "You should always do the best you can do no matter what it is."

By the time Aunt Lillian finished talking to us, we were home.

The Old African

The following Sunday, we stayed home after the afternoon service ended at Slades Chapel. Late that afternoon, there was a definite shift in the wind. Cooler, drier air was blowing in from the west. DePapa sat in his front yard under the tree fragrant with wisteria. We could see Patricia, Beverly, and Diane playing across the street. We could hear their singsong voices:

"Miss Mary Mack, Mack, Mack

All dressed in black, black, black

She asked her mother, mother, mother

For fifteen cents, cents, cents,

To see the elephant, elephant, elephant

Jump the fence, fence, fence,

He jumped so high, high, high,

He touched the sky, sky, sky,

He didn't come back, back, back,

Til the Fourth of July, ly, ly."

I saw DePapa looking at the girls, smiling. When he saw me looking at him, he stopped smiling and said in somewhat of a stern voice, "You see those girls over there singing like that, well in the old days, people kept the Sabbath. You could not work, cook, play, or anything. Everything had to be done before sundown the night before the Sabbath. On Sunday, people stayed in church all day and did not mind. Times sure have changed from the old days when I was a child."

I knew then that DePapa was going to start talking about the "old African." I had heard this story so many times that I could recite it by heart; yet I never got tired of hearing my grandfather repeat it.

DePapa began, "Ike, I've told Johnny this story and I want you to know it, too. It is part of our history, part of who we are. Our first ancestor on my father's side of the family to be brought here from Africa was named Tamishan. As my grandfather told me and his father told him, Tamishan was of noble birth. He was a proud man. He could read and write from the Koran and could speak seven different languages. He came to the attention of his slave master, old Waightstill Avery. Avery and other slaveholders were also impressed with Tamishan's abilities and would listen to him read from the Koran. But Tamishan never accepted his lot as a slave and often encouraged other slaves to feel the same way. Soon he became known as a troublemaker. When he asked Avery if he could return to Africa in exchange for four Africans, Avery agreed, with certain conditions. One condition was that he had to be taken to Charleston by William Walton, a merchant who traded in slaves, and two, that the captain of the ship was not to let Tamishan go ashore alone. All agreed to the terms and Walton took Tamishan to Charleston where he boarded a ship for West Africa.

"During the voyage, the captain and Tamishan had long conversations.

Because Tamishan had so impressed the captain with his knowledge and skills, when they arrived on the West coast of Africa, the captain allowed Tamishan to go alone into the interior in search of Africans. He returned in four days with four hundred dollars in gold dust, the value of four slaves. He told the captain to give the money to his former master, that he could not sell his people into slavery."

DePapa continued, deep in thought as if he was reliving the story he was telling. "Tamishan lived on Swans Pond on the Johns River. Old Avery was the largest plantation holder in the county. Tamishan lived on the plantation, took a wife, and had one son by the name of Big Alf. Big Alf, or 'Alfred,' also had a son named Alfred. Alfred, the son, married Clarissa and had Isaac, my father. Slavery life was hard. People worked all the time, but our families were kept intact. When emancipation time came, we were free to go and come as we saw fit. Papa and Grandpapa secured land on what is West Burkemont Avenue today. They changed their name to "Fleming" because Avery was a slave name. They chose Fleming because they knew a white man and his family with that name. The Flemings had a reputation for being fair and honest and were not slaveholders. So that's how we became Flemings and not Averys.

"I remember every time Grandpa would see his former owner coming down Burkemont Avenue, Grandpa would take great pleasure in sitting on his porch like a man of leisure, showing his former owner that he was his own boss, now. This used to greatly irritate old man Avery," DePapa said.

DePapa told us always to remember that: "We were not and could not be slaves so long as we knew who we were. We come from a proud line of Africans of noble birth. We kept our pride because we know who we are. You should do the same. Never let any one mistreat you. Take up for your rights as a human being.

"Now, my wife Becky, your grandmother, her family history is different. Their lives were tied to that of their owner." And DePapa began to tell us about his wife's family history. "Your grandmother, Rebecca, died in 1948. She was the daughter of Lucy Ann Avery, who was the daughter of her master A. Hamilton Erwin and his slave, Myra. Myra's mother was part Indian, white and colored from Virginia. Hamp Erwin purchased Myra when she was 12. Together, they had five children, four girls and a boy.

"When the Civil War came and Union forces came into Morganton, the boy burned his father's barn and escaped with the Union forces to Tennessee. He was taken to Camp Campbell up in Ohio, and then to Chicago, where he settled. Fifty years passed before he was reunited with his sisters."

DePapa turned to me, "Your mama's people, the Woodards and the Lytles, and the Erwins all trace their heritage back to these sisters through Myra and her master/husband, old Hamp Erwin. Your Uncle George used to travel with his grandmother, Lucy Ann, in a buckboard to the old homestead to visit her white relatives. He always had to remain outside on the wagon. He told me that his grandmother would always be crying when she came out of the house. I think that there must be a real love-hate relationship between blacks and whites who are kin. Racial etiquette in the South demanded racial separation, but we all know the circumstances by which we became related. Sometimes guilt and shame are manifested as cruelty."

DePapa went on, "The Erwins may have been ashamed of the relationship, but old Hamp Erwin was not. He gave all of his children some land. Lucy Ann, Becky's mother, got her fair share and Becky had a good deal of land as part of her share when I married her. We have given some for the colored school and the colored cemetery. All of our children got lots and we sold some to people who needed land to build homes."

I asked, "DePapa, you mean that Big Momma gave the land for our school?"

And he replied, "Well, she got about nothin' for the land, so we consider it a donation. We must always remember our heritage. Remember who you are and be proud. People tried to hide our history from us, but my father and his father and his father's father told this story over and over. This story is written down somewhere, but white folks won't give it to me. I asked Attorney Sam Ervin about it one day and he told me that he didn't know anything about it. I know it's there, though, because my father told me it was written in a book."

DePapa told us the story of Tamishan often as if to ensure that we would remember. During this telling, Ike was very quiet, but I am sure that he, too, would remember and be influenced by our heritage.

The Racial Incident

That same week that we heard the story of Tamishan, we encountered our first racial incident in Morganton. Ike and I had done very little during most of the summer to entertain ourselves; we had been so busy working. So, when Jimmy asked if we wanted to go to the movies to see "King Kong," we both agreed.

Morganton was a very interesting community. All places of public accommodations were segregated. If you chose not to go to any of those places, you were pretty much insulated from racial discrimination or racial affronts. Since Morganton was not a heavily segregated town residentially, one generally had to have some contacts with the white community. Unless you were a black minister, your work environment always brought you into some contacts with whites. Daddy tried to keep us from being placed in humiliating positions. There were some things we could do and some things we could not. We were not permitted to be caddies for white golfers. I never quite understood this rule because our friends made a lot of money caddying for white golfers. We could not eat food on the street and we definitely could not go up to a "colored" carryout window and purchase food. We were told to mind our own business and to stay out of trouble.

When it came to "trouble," Daddy did not mind voicing his support for the Reverend Martin Luther King, Jr. Daddy subscribed to *Jet, Ebony, The Afro-American,* and *The Norfork Journal and Guide* to keep up with the colored news, especially with Dr. King's movement. Daddy also watched Dr. King on national television. Daddy, like his father, was a "race man." He knew that Dr. King would bring about great change throughout the South, change that he would see in his lifetime.

Daddy regularly kept up with the news, especially events surrounding the Montgomery Bus Boycott. He had great respect for Rosa Parks for refusing to give up her seat to a white man and move to the back of the bus. Daddy said that she was already in the back of the bus in the colored section. The bus driver had moved the sign back a row to increase the number of available seats for white people. They wanted her to stand and let the white man sit in the colored section. All of that took place the previous December and the boycott was still going strong in August of 1956. All of the black papers carried news of the boycott every week.

Daddy did not like to do things that might suggest that one went along with segregation. That is why he was ambivalent when it came to letting us go to the movies. We thought he was cheap because we had to pay only a dime and all the kids went to the show on Saturdays to see the matinee as well as the on-going attractions. We could never keep up with any of the serials because we could only go the movies when Daddy felt like we could go.

We thought it was a matter of money, but that was not the issue. Most of the time we had our own money. Many times, we would tell Patricia that we were going to the movies and she would automatically ask Mother or Daddy if Jimmy and Johnny were going to the movies, could she go? Most of the time they would say, "Nobody is going to the movies!" But once in a while they would not object and they still would not let Patricia go—she was a girl.

The movie theater was called the "Mimosa." Practically everything in Morganton was at one time or another named after the Mimosa tree. The Mimosa tree is beautiful, with small feathery leaves and the most delicate pink fuzzy blossoms. The Mimosa Theater was located next to the Caldwell Hotel in the center of downtown, near the town square and across from the Courthouse. To get to the movies, we walked east on West Concord, north on Anderson Street for one block, and east on West Union until we reached the center of town. We passed the Caldwell Hotel and went up the alley between the hotel and the theater. Midway up the alley on the side of the theater was the colored entrance. We had to climb a flight of stairs to the second level where the colored balcony was located. The ticket counter where we purchased our tickets for the movie and popcorn and sodas sat on the landing. We then walked up a center hall split by a seven-foot wall which was the dividing line between the colored and white balcony sections of the theater. Whites had four-fifths of the theater for the whites-only section—the entire first floor and half of the balcony. The remainder was for colored only.

Most of the time there was harmony between blacks and whites. Sometimes, whites in the balcony would throw paper or cups over the wall. Blacks almost never threw anything over the balcony. If this happened, management immediately came up to reprimand and threaten the black audience. Generally, each group stayed in their place without discord.

It was a warm summer night when Jimmy, Ike, and I left the theater. We cut across the courthouse lawn as we usually did and walked up West Union without incident. We again cut across the vacant lot at the corner of Union and Anderson and walked down Concord. As we passed Miss Celi's house, a car with four or five white boys in it came racing down Concord and threw several soft drink bottles out the window at us as they yelled, "Niggers, get off the street!"

Completely taken by surprise, we automatically yelled back, "Who you calling 'nigger,' you peckerwood!" Boy, did that put a damper on the evening! The car was quickly out of sight, having turned right onto Circle Street. There were just a few white families living on Circle Street. As we continued walking home, all sorts of things crossed my mind. I had heard about racial violence in other places in the South, but not here in Morganton. We certainly had not experienced any racial incidents. I didn't understand why anyone would want to hit us with bottles and call us "niggers." How could those white boys hate us when they didn't even know us? As we walked home quietly in the dark, I was trying to understand race relations in our small town. Almost everyone I knew worked with or rather for white people. Yet, no one had any white friends. Morganton, like other communities, was segregated, but we lived next door to white families. Often segregation was invisible, otherwise, how could black women do the most intimate things for white people like cooking their food, cleaning their homes, washing their clothes and nursing their children and still be segregated.

As I thought about racism, I remembered the night Dad came home and told us that Walt Greene, his white employer at the frame shop, had invited us to dinner at his house. I couldn't believe that mother and daddy had been invited to the home of a white family for a social event. I know that I had never eaten with white people before. Of course, I had eaten a sandwich on the back porch of a white home where I worked, but that was as close as I had come.

I thought of Walt Greene because he was a kind man who had given Dad a job making picture frames when Dad needed extra work. Mr. Greene had a studio on West Union Street above a men's clothing store. I often went up the stairs to meet Dad after work only to find him and Mr. Greene working together in the back. It never occurred to me that they might have become friends.

On the night we were to visit the Greenes' home, Dad had us put on our best clothes—not the Sunday best, but more like the first-day-of-school best. We did wear our Sunday shoes. As we drove to the Greene's house, Dad kept saying "Don't say anything unless you are spoken to." That was already a well-known rule in our house: Speak when you are spoken to and come when you are called. Dad seemed a little nervous, while Mother was quite calm. I was just hungry.

The Greenes lived in a long, white frame ranch house on the far end of West Union Street. The area was across the road from Riverside Drive, where many of the well-to-do whites lived. The house was on a lot that sloped down to the street. It also sat behind a large grouping of trees that made the house invisible from the street in the spring and summer. In the fall, the lawn was covered with fallen tree leaves several inches thick. I knew the yard well because on one occasion Dad agreed to rake the leaves for Mr. Greene on Thanksgiving Day. Of course, he made Jimmy and me help. We started early that morning while mother was home cooking the Thanksgiving turkey. Even though it was cold, thinking of the feast at home encouraged us to get the job done quickly.

The Greenes' yard was so large and there were so many leaves, it seemed that Thanksgiving would be over before we were finished. We raked and raked until almost five 5:00 that afternoon. Jimmy and I reasoned that everybody in town must have eaten their dinner. I tried to keep my spirits up, but Jimmy did not mind showing how angry he was. He wanted to go home, so he began slacking off. He worked slower and slower until Dad said, "Johnny and I are going home and eat dinner when we finish. If you are not finished, you can just stay here until those leaves are raked and carried around back." Boy was that enough to get Jimmy moving. By five forty-five we were all done. It was just as well because it was dark and we could no longer see the leaves.

As we drove down the Greenes' driveway the evening of our dinner invitation, I kept thinking about that cold Thanksgiving Day. Then I heard Dad say, "Watch you manners, and Johnny, don't talk so much."

Walt Greene and his wife greeted us in front of their garage and escorted us to the back where he had already started the fire in the outdoor grill. Walt Greene's daughter and young son joined us. The adults sat at one table and the children at another. The evening passed swiftly. The hamburgers were good, but I did not like the potato salad. It was hot and had vinegar in it. I ate it anyway because I knew that there were hungry children in China.

After dinner, we carried our plates to the kitchen. Remembering Dad telling me to watch my manners, I offered to help wash the dishes. Mrs. Greene said, "Oh, no, we have a dish washer." All the way home Patricia kept laughing and repeating, "Can I help you wash the dishes, Can I help you wash the dishes....Oh no, We have a dishwasher."

As Jimmy, Ike and I walked up our driveway toward our house, just remembering the kindness of the Greenes that evening was enough to make me believe that all white people were not like the white boys who called us "niggers" and hated us just because we were colored. When we got home, we told Mother and Daddy what had happened. There was nothing anyone could do about it. It was just another ugly event in the life of a segregated town.

Ike and I talked a long time that night. I asked him, "Do you want to go to a integrated school?"

Ike replied, "You know I've thought a lot about that since the Supreme Court said that we had to go to school with whites two years ago, but nothing has happened since then. I haven't heard anything in Durham about blacks and whites going to school together. The only school integration I see is on the news on television when some little Negro children try to enroll in a white school and white folks are yelling 'Niggers go home!' "

"I never thought about attending school with white students," I said. "When we heard that we would have to integrate, we all said that we did not want to go to school with white students. We are happy at Olive Hill. I know that we get used books from the white school; we don't get their old books until they finish with them and get all new books. Then they send their old books over to us. We will be getting our band uniforms from the white high school too, but we have teachers who care about us and we don't have to worry about people calling us names."

Ike said, "That's all I need is to get into trouble at a white school! You know, I have a hard enough time just paying attention at my colored school!"

"Yeah, I don't need a white teacher calling me 'dummy' if I just happen to be thinking about something else more important," I added.

Ike said, "Me neither!"

"Ike," I said, "do you remember the story of Tamishan that DePapa was telling us?"

"Yes, why?" he replied.

"Well, I think DePapa was trying to let us know that we can overcome anything in life including racism. Tonight we had that incident with the white boys throwing bottles at us and calling us 'nigger.' You know that was nothing compared to what DePapa and his father and grandfather had to go through in the old days. They were slaves, man! Can you imagine someone else owning you? You have to work all the time for nothing? You have to ask for permission to do everything. You couldn't even travel to see your relatives if they lived on another plantation unless you had permission. You had no rights. Yet, DePapa is a strong man and he must come from strong people. White people in this town respect him. Some people call him 'Uncle Dee,' but most call him 'Mr. Dee.' Did you know that DePapa votes?"

"No," said Ike, "but I know people like the Spauldings vote. I think it's because they have money and are Republicans."

"Yeah," I went on, "DePapa is a Republican and voted for President Eisenhower both times. I know because DePapa sat in our house and watched the Republican Convention. I have already decided that I want to be like DePapa when I grow up. He is quiet, but he does not take anything off anybody. He is his own man. I think people will respect you if you demand respect. And DePapa demands respect."

With that, Ike said, "But I still don't want to go to school with no white kids..." and he was asleep.

"Goodnight, Ike," I said.

CHAPTER VII:
SUMMER ENDS

"Where has the summer gone?" I thought to myself. June and July were gone and August was almost over. We continued to work long hours for Mr. Wilford, but our work was changing with the end of the growing season. The work was more monotonous now. While we still had our routine of collecting slop from the State Hospital and feeding the animals, once all of that was done, we had to start harvesting the corn. Now I knew the meaning of "from sun-up to sundown," which was the way slaves and sharecroppers always worked. We pulled the corn ears from the stalks, shucked the ears, and threw them into bushel baskets. When the baskets were full, we emptied them into the back of the pick up truck. When the truck was full, we took the corn to two storage areas. One was located in the back of Mr. Wilford's house and was used for the feed for both the hogs and chickens. The other was in the back of Rev. Carson's house and was used to store feed for his chickens.

All summer long we gathered vegetables as they became ripe. Everybody in the neighborhood was canning; it was like a mini-factory. What people did not grow in their own gardens was given to them by Mr. Wilford. We carried food to Miss Mae Lee, the Clarks, Miss Mae Scott, the Tates, to whoever needed food and even to some who didn't. Everybody got some of the bounty.

During those days, we had plenty of time to talk and think. I told Ike how Aunt Lillian always let us help her can. Our favorite job was canning "chow chow." It was an all day job. Aunt Lillian would start off by washing the bottles and the lids. Then she would sterilize all the bottles and lids by boiling them. Meanwhile, Patricia, Tommy and I collected the ingredients for the chow chow. We took the outer leaves off six or eight cabbages. Then we peeled onions and cut up bell peppers—green, yellow and red, which gave the chow chow its color. Aunt Lillian had a hand food grinder, which she attached to the large oak dining room table. I never knew what special seasoning Aunt Lillian put in the chow chow. Our job was to do the grinding. We started off with the cabbage, then the peppers, and finally the onions, which always brought tears to our eyes. By the time we were finished, we had two large dishpans full of chopped vegetables. Aunt Lillian placed both dishpans on the stove and added lots of sugar, vinegar, and some yellow powder, which gave the chow chow a yellow color. She then filled the jars with the mixture and placed the lids and rings on the jars. She boiled water and placed the jars into the vigorously boiling water for maybe 30 minutes. When she finished, we knew that the jars were sealed because they "popped."

Mother stopped canning a lot of stuff after Daddy purchased a freezer. Most of the vegetables she put up were placed in little freezer bags or in plastic containers. That first year we owned it, Daddy went crazy buying stuff for the freezer. Every week he would bring home a bushel of peaches or strawberries or green beans. Always something. We loved to prepare strawberries for freezing because we ate one for every two we cleaned.

That same year Daddy purchased the freezer, he also purchased a side of beef. I heard him tell Mother, "We could raise our own beef for what that side of beef cost!" Mother wanted to know where we would raise a cow, since we didn't have room in our yard for anything else. But before the end of September, Daddy had purchased a young steer and had it delivered to our cousins, the Pooles, over in Glen Alpine. We kids never saw the calf until spring, when Daddy announced that it was ready for slaughter. One Saturday, Daddy announced, "Johnny! You and Jimmy go get in the car." Daddy was never one for telling you needless information. We did not know what was up until we got to our destination.

We drove up to Miss Poole's in our 1951 four-door sky blue Plymouth. Miss Poole had a small farm on which she raised cows and chickens. She sold eggs, butter, and buttermilk to friends and neighbors. The farm was not large. There was a large two-story house at the end of a dirt driveway that came off the highway. The house had been painted once, but it was difficult to tell when. The meadow was fenced in and sloped down toward the creek. The field had as many rocks in it as it had blades of grass. This lack of grass in the pasture did not bother Daddy. He brought in feed for our calf the whole time it was in the country. We walked down to the pasture where the calf was. It was bigger than what we thought, but it was still a calf. I think that it was costing Daddy too much money and he decided to kill it early. He brought the car to the edge of the pasture, got out, and put a rope around the neck of the calf. He pulled it over to the car and tried to get it to go into the back. It stopped and would not move an inch. After about half an hour of trying to coach the balky calf into the car without success, Daddy said, "There's only one thing to do, boys. You'll have to walk it back to our house in Morganton."

Ike started to laugh out loud as I told him the story of walking the calf to town. "Johnny, I can see you and Jimmy now, trying to pull that cow along the highway."

I corrected him, "It wasn't a cow; it was a steer."

Continuing the story, I said, "Walking the cow back to Morganton meant that Jimmy and I had to walk alongside the calf on the berm, while Daddy slowly drove the car, with lights flashing, behind us. All I could think about was that I hoped none of our friends would see us. Kids were always looking for ammunition to use against each other. I remember the time that I was visiting at Steve Robinson's house and his mother had left the mail on the breakfast table. I just happened to look down and saw a catalogue for women with big feet. I had never thought about Miss Robinson having particularly big feet, until I saw the caption on the catalogue. It said, "Shoes to Fit Any Size from 12 AAAA to 17 EEEEE." If that was not teasin' material, I don't know what was!

So, rather than be concerned about the long walk, the heat, or even getting hit by a car, all I thought about was not wanting anyone I knew to see me walking with this calf! I walked in the grass holding one end of the rope, which was attached to the head of the calf. Jimmy held the other end of the rope and walked on the roadway. Daddy followed us in his car with two wheels on the berm and two on the road. Cars and trucks would pull up behind Daddy and pass as soon as the coast was clear. Large trucks frightened the calf. He tried to lunge forward several times, straining our young arms in our desperate attempt to hold onto him. The midday sun was awfully hot, but I didn't mind—my cap was already pulled down over my face to prevent recognition by friend or foe! Somehow, we finally managed to get the calf home and staked out in the back yard.

Daddy said, "The Freezer Locker can't slaughter the calf until next week. Therefore, you'll have to care for it until then." We fed him out of one of Mother's mop buckets. We called him "Toby." Yes, we had named our pet and a pet it was. We washed it, and dried it, Patricia combed its hair, and we gave it food and water. We tried to train it to attack when we waved a red blanket in front of its head.

When Saturday came, we were not prepared to take our Toby to be slaughtered. We tried to talk Dad into letting us keep it and pretend like it was a big dog. But of course, that got us nowhere.

This time Daddy decided that we had a better chance of getting Toby into the car if the back seat were removed. Once the back seat was taken out, we found several quarters and dimes underneath. Daddy pulled on the rope that was attached around Toby's neck. He said that he would guide Toby into the back as we pushed him from behind. With a lot of tugging and pushing, we actually finally did get Toby into the back seat, and off we went to the Freezer Locker.

I said, "You know, Ike, I know you won't believe this, but the next time we saw Toby, he was between hamburger buns."

And Ike laughed.

The Case of the "Hollow" Theft

By the end of August, Ike and I were pretty adept at getting our chores done. The quicker we completed our assigned tasks, the more time we had to ride the horse! We had gotten to be good riders. Ike would ride the horse to the barn and I would ride it back to Mr. Wilford's back yard. We would continue doing this until we saw Mr. Wilford and then we would pretend that we were just then getting around to riding the horse down to the barn for the evening.

As the season was ending, we no longer worked from 6:00 in the morning to 8:00 or 9:00 at night. Sometimes we would manage to get everything done that needed to be done that day and be ready to go home around 7:00 p.m. By the time we finished bathing and eating, we would still have time to sit in the front yard with DePapa, Aunt Lillian, Mother and Daddy, and other neighbors or relatives who came by that evening. Will, of course, was a regular. But Will would come by only after he had made his "rounds" for the night. He traveled to Rudell's, Mr. Gaither's, Ed Powell's, and wherever else he thought he could collect the "news," before heading back to Aunt Lillian's house with his embellished report.

We had heard earlier in the summer about somebody stealing food and other things from people around town, but had not kept up with the latest events. Usually, by the time we finished our work, took our baths and ate dinner, it was time for bed. It was mainly on Sundays that we could sit in the front yard with the rest of the family and enjoy the summer nights. We had no idea how bad the thefts had actually gotten and that people were actually frightened.

That evening, Will rushed up the hill to DePapa's house. Now, Will was a good deal overweight, and by the time he was in front of Miss Hester's house, he huffing and puffing as he began to relate what had happened.

He kept repeating, "The police. . ., the police. . ."

We all stopped and looked at him. We knew this time that he had something important to say—something more than the usual gossip he carried from house to house.

"The police are in Jonesboro trying to determine who broke into several houses over there, icluding Ed Powell's house!" Will exclaimed.

Ed Powell's house was actually in the hollow. His land bordered on the creek that ran through the hollow. He had little houses for his animals all over his place. Ed Powell had lots of chickens, some hogs, lots of dogs, and heaven knows what else he kept among the many little outhouses, shacks, plus his own small house, which had been added onto three or four different times. Ed Powell never seemed to have a regular job. He went about town collecting whatever he thought he might be able to use, trade, sell, or just retain for future use. Strewn about around his property were bicycles, an old car, steel mattress springs, wagon wheels, barrels, various garden tools, toys, pots and pans, wheelbarrows and an old buckboard. And those were just a few of the items one could immediately identify! He was a natural-born "packrat."

Ed claimed he was a cousin of my grandmother. Momma never denied it; nor did she claim he was kin. She would just say, "Ed Powell claims to be our cousin, but I don't know." And she left it at that. But he would always tip his hat and say, "Good afternoon, Cousin Margaret."

He certainly was a nice enough guy. He never bothered anyone. He was married and had two daughters. One day he was found in the dumpster behind the super market. While on his usual inspection for anything useful, he had fallen in and could not get out. Daddy said that he had probably had one too many that night which explained why he couldn't climb out. It must have been late Sunday night because no one heard him call for help. It was not until Monday that he was found and rescued.

Will said, "Ed Powell called the police when he found that someone had broken into his house and taken dinner right off the stove. Someone also took some bread, coffee, soda, cereal, and sugar. They found some tracks leading to the creek, but that's where they ended."

This news got everybody's attention, including mine and Ike's.

Daddy asked, "What did the police say?"

Will said, "The police are treating this like a single incident. They don't seem to understand that this had been happening ever since the 'goat man' came to town."

Mr. Wilford, Miss Hester, and Miss Lucille all walked over after hearing the excitement in Will's voice, and Mr. Wilford, who never socialized, asked Will, "What happened?" He had noticed the police car up at the top of the hill in front of Ed Powell's house.

Will continued his report excitedly, "Ed Powell called the police after finding out that someone broke into his house and robbed him. You know that someone broke into several houses in Jonesboro and in this neighborhood."

Mr. Wilford, somewhat reluctantly contributing to the conversation, said, "We," meaning he, Ike and I, "have noticed strange footprints coming up from the creek into the garden, and we've been missing lots of vegetables, too; but I assumed that animals from the hollow were taking them. Most of the things taken were from the side of the garden next to the hollow. That's the only place that had strange footprints and missing vegetables."

DePapa said, "Why would anyone be stealing food? There's so much around."

Sounding like a broken record, Will said, "Well, you know it started this summer when the 'goat man' came to town. That's when things started to be missing from other houses in the neighborhood."

As the grownups continued to debate the issue, Ike and I walked into the house and upstairs to sort this thing out.

We thought, "Who would be stealing from neighbors? Why food? Why certain people and not others?" And as we pondered these questions, a pattern began to emerge.

I pointed out, "Ike, all of the thefts occurred at places bordering on the hollow!"

"You're right! That's it. That's the key!" he exclaimed.

I said, "Ed Powell's house is the house farthest from Concord Street. The Tate's house, Miss Frankie's house, and Miss Mae Lee's house are all close to the hollow. And so is Mr. Wilford's garden!"

"Hey, Johnny, didn't you tell me that Billy Tate saw Peg Leg Jim though his bedroom window earlier in the summer?" Ike asked.

"Yeah, it was earlier in the summer."

Ike said, "Will might not be right about the 'goat man.' It might be Peg Leg Jim. Then there's only one thing for us to do! If Peg Leg Jim is doing the stealing, we have to go up into the hollow at night and catch him with the goods. We have to catch him red-handed."

"Oooh no, not me," I shuddered, "I'm not about to go into that hollow at night!"

"What's the matter, you scared?" Ike teased.

"Me? I ain't scared of nothing!" I boldly protested.

"Then it's settled. We will go find this Peg Leg Jim tomorrow night." Ike sounded so confident that it ended any further discussion.

The last thing that I wanted to do at night was to go up into that hollow north of Concord Street to find someone or something that I wasn't looking for but I did not want Ike to know that I was afraid to go in the hollow at night. Ike didn't know that I was afraid of stuff, a lot of stuff. If Ike had not been there, I would never have stayed at Aunt Lillian's upstairs by myself at night for all the money in the world. Whenever I had to go into Aunt Lillian's house by myself at night with no one home, I would turn on all the lights, do what I had to do, and get out fast.

The only time that I really was not afraid was when I was with Jimmy. From the earliest that I can remember, Jimmy was my security. We slept in the same room on that little double cot from the time we moved into our house. Jimmy never seemed to be afraid of anything. He was the oldest. He was the boss. He knew more than I did. He could explain everything, make me understand, or just make it right.

If I had a nightmare, Mother would say, "You had a bad dream, go back to sleep," but Jimmy would tell me a story and make me feel better. My favorite story was "Pinto Beans and Cornbread." He always started, "Pinto

Beans and Cornbread had a fight last night. Pinto Beans knocked Cornbread out of sight. . ." Before he could finish the story, I was asleep.

When Jimmy went to kindergarten, he had to go by himself. When it was time for me to go, I went with Jimmy. Jimmy would protect me. Every day on the way to the kindergarten on Spa Street just before we got to Miss O'Neil's school, a dog would come out from the under this lady's porch and bark at us as if it were going to bite us. As we would approach the house, I would move to Jimmy's right side, so that if the dog attacked someone, it would be Jimmy. And when we went home, I would walk on Jimmy's left side.

When Mother bought us twin beds and moved us into her and Daddy's old room, that was the first time I had to sleep alone in a bed. I was always afraid at night. Even so, I loved to watch horror movies or "The Twilight Zone," and by bedtime I would be just about terrified. When the lights were out, I could see all sorts of things moving in the dark. Every shadow was menacing. I believed every ghost story I'd ever heard. And now, even though I was 12 years old, to think that I would be going up into that dark old hollow at night was beyond belief. Not even Jimmy went into the hollow at night! Needless to say, I did not sleep well at all that night. I was restless, just thinking about what Ike wanted to do.

The next day passed quickly, way too quickly for me. I was still scared. Even Bible stories use to frighten me. Whenever I heard the sound of a loud horn or siren, I thought it was the Angel Gabriel announcing the coming of Judgment Day. If there was a particularly bright sunset with fiery red clouds in the sky, it was a just another sign that Judgment Day was coming that evening and some part of the earth was already engulfed in flames. I believed as much in eternal damnation as I believed in Heaven.

In spite of these irrational fears, if Ike was determined to go through with our plans, I would have to go, too. I could never let Ike know that I was afraid. I tried to put these scary thoughts aside, as Ike and I prepared for the night's adventure in our room. I had taken two of Daddy's flashlights from his toolbox. I had my boots and Ike wore the boots Mr. Wilford had given him at the beginning of the summer. Ike told me to get a camera so we could document whatever we found. I had five unexposed shots left on my box camera. I thought that that should be plenty.

With all our plans in place, we went to bed at 10:00 p.m. Our plan was to wake up at midnight to begin our investigation. We were sound asleep by the time Aunt Lillian got around to turningoff the hall light.

Ike said, "It's midnight. Time to go."

Trying not to wake Aunt Lillian (she was a light sleeper – it wasn't easy!), we walked slowly down the steps, through the dining room and out the backdoor. We walked down Concord Street as far as Miss Frankie's. This was the edge of what I had always considered to be "safe territory." We cut to the back of Miss Frankie's and then through Mr. Wilford's garden, behind Miss Mae Lee's house. Down the steep slope and into the hollow we went. We decided that we would follow the creek through the culvert that ran under Concord Street—into the danger zone, "No Man's Land."

There had been a full moon when we started, but by the time we slowly moved up the hill, much of the moon's light began to be obscured by thickening clouds. There were menacing shadows everywhere. The tall trees and long thick vines, allies in the light, now turned into long cords of rope ready to be used in unknown terrifying ways to entrap us forever.

We heard the eerie sounds of the night—the babbling brook, the croaking of the frogs, and the constant noise of summer crickets. A bat gently flew by our heads, contributing to my feelings that we were not alone. The creek narrowed as we climbed the hill. We could not see the Tate house because naturally, the Tates had all gone to bed and turned off all the lights. I thought, "Here we are, the only fools out after midnight." The Tate house was our last contact with the civilized world.

In the distance, on the side of the hill, we saw the flicker of a fire. We approached slowly and cautiously. We saw the outline of this old one-room shack, with lots of junk around it. I whispered to Ike, "Maybe we should do our investigation from here."

But he said, "Oh Johnny, we can't see nothin' from here! We have to get much closer to find any evidence."

We moved closer, slowly, quietly, cautiously. Ike first, then me as we crept closer and closer. We had come to the corner of the house. We looked for an opening to peer in, but finding none, we moved along the clapboard wall and approached the fire.

"Get down!" Ike hissed. "I think I see something."

"What?"

"I'm not sure. I think it's someone down by the fire. It's hard to tell."

"Let me see," I said nervously, trying to peer around Ike.

"OK, but be quiet," he whispered.

I crawled around in front of Ike on my hands and knees over the damp ground. I slowly peered around the corner of the shack until I could see the flicker of flames. I couldn't see Old Jim or anything else. We waited silently, daring not to move

Then, suddenly out of the darkness something hard and crooked wrapped, then tightened around my neck and yanked me down the hill.

"He-elp!!" I let out a scream at the top of my lungs! I had never felt such fear, though I had certainly been afraid in the past. I wanted to run, but where? I could not see. We had lost our flashlights. I felt warm water slide down the inside of my leg.

Before I could yell again or do anything else, something picked Ike up and threw him down the hill. He landed just to my left and whispered, "Do you see anything?"

"No, do you?"

"No."

A strange voice came out of the dark still night, "Who are you and what do you want on my property!?"

Without our flashlights, we could see only a silhouette against the light of the flickering fire. I thought, "It's a wild man with hair all over his head and face!" He stood there with the raised cane that he had used to pull me to the ground. I could see the outline of one leg and when I looked to the other, I saw a wooden leg that extended from the knee joint down to the ground.

"Look out! It's Peg Leg Jim!" I shrieked.

"Where? Where? I don't see him," Ike exclaimed.

Just then a cold hand grabbed me by the neck. I could hardly catch my breath as I screamed, "Ike, Ike, where are you?"

Old Jim had grabbed Ike as suddenly as he had grabbed me. He was holding us both in mid air. He walked slowly over to what appeared to be this bottomless pit. We always heard that Peg Leg Jim had a pit where he dropped children who dared to come on his property. He leaned over the pit and dropped Ike down into a sea of darkness. I could hear him scream for help. I knew that I would be next. I hollered at the top of my voice for Ike. My worst nightmare was to be left hanging on a narrow cliff or any precipice. Jim had me by the neck as I hung over the pit. Then Jim let go of my neck, and I was in a free fall rapidly approaching the bottom. Just before I crashed, I felt two hands shaking me.

"Wake up, wake up!" I heard this distant voice repeat time and time again, wake up!

I could see Ike's silhouette, as he sat on the edge of the bed, framed by the glow of the streetlight shining through the window.

Ike said, "Johnny, you must have had a bad dream. You kept screaming, 'Don't drop me! Don't drop me!' You were screaming so loudly, you woke me up. I'm surprised you didn't wake up everybody in the house."

By this time I was sitting straight up in bed. I told Ike, "I dreamed that we went looking for Old Peg Leg Jim. It was so real. Jim looked just like Billy Tate said. He had long wild hair that was completely white. His skin was dark and he didn't have any teeth, except for one in front and one on the side. When he grinned, he was a horrible sight. His clothes were torn. His left leg was cut off at the knee and he wore a wooden peg. He did not have a shoe on his right foot either. Ike, my dream was so real. We tried to run, but even with a peg leg, old Jim caught up with us and dropped us in his pit. It was so real!"

"Johnny, I guess we both fell asleep. Looks like you made the trip in your dream, but it was only a dream. You're got to face up to your fears and not let them get out of control. Otherwise, your fears will control you. I learned that lesson when I thought I was going to reform school," Ike said.

"Ike, going into that hollow to face Peg Leg Jim was my worse nightmare even though I know it was just a dream. The funny thing about dreams, when you wake up, it's as if you have already been there. Real life can't be any worse than what I experienced in my dream, Ike."

It was nice just to be able to talk to someone who could understand my fears and not judge me. I did not want Ike to go home. I drifted off to sleep thinking about all of our experiences during the summer....

Ike Goes Home

The end of August had come too soon. Today, Friday, was Ike's last day of working for Mr. Wilford. I started to think, "When Ike leaves, I don't want to work for Mr. Wilford just by myself!" The fun of working was having someone to work with. With Ike gone, work would be drudgery. I had to think about what I was going to do. Labor Day was coming up on Monday. Uncle John and Uncle Louie would be coming in tomorrow, Saturday, to pick up Ike. What would I tell Mr. Wilford?

That Friday we got up bright and early. Aunt Lillian had already made breakfast and was sitting in the dining room, talking to DePapa and drinking her second cup of coffee. They were talking about Martin Luther King. It seemed everybody was talking about Dr. King and what people were calling the "Civil Rights Movement."

DePapa said, "Dr. King is going to make white people sit up and listen to what black people have to say. I've lived in two centuries, over 80 years. During my entire lifetime, black people in this country have been treated like second-class citizens. White people have never respected the rights of blacks in this country. That's why my great, great granddaddy left and went back to Africa when he had the chance."

Looking up at us as we entered the room, he continued, "I am glad that you boys have come down stairs. This is a new day! Dr. King will make white folks pay attention to black folks. I may not live to see it, but you boys will. You'll live in a society where it does not matter that you are colored. You'll be judged on your ability to do a job, any job, not just a Negro job. You boys will be able to work anywhere you want, live anywhere you want, marry anyone you want. You'll get the same pay for the same work as whites. Dr. King will bring this about. I can feel it. He is the one we have been looking for all these years to lead us. He is not afraid to lead. Now, you boys pay attention to what is happening in Montgomery and other parts of the South. Things are changing all over and they will change in North Carolina and eventually even in Morganton. You boys must be ready. You have to be prepared to take advantage of what will come your way. You'll have opportunities we never dreamed of having. You have to be ready.

"You boys know that the elections are only a few months off. Do you know who General Eisenhower is?"

Ike said, "Yes sir, he is the President."

DePapa said, "That's right. He is the President and he's running for a second term. He's also a Republican and I always vote Republican. You know that President Lincoln freed the slaves and he was a Republican. With Martin Luther King putting so much pressure on the government, it will be Eisenhower, a Republican, who will help bring about changes in race relations."

And he repeated for emphasis, "You boys better be ready for change!"

"This has been a great summer for you boys. Mr. Wilford was kind enough to let you work for him. I know that you've learned a lot and have learned the value of hard work. You should continue to work hard in school. Listen to your parents, your teachers, and all those who have your best interests at heart. This is a new day and you should be ready for it. Whatever you decide to do in life, do the very best you can."

"I will," Ike said, inspired.

And I said, "I will too, DePapa."

We finished our eggs and grits and were off. As usual, Mr. Wilford was waiting for us in his truck. For the last time, we drove over to the State Hospital to pick up the buckets of slop. On the way back, we passed by the old Avery Plantation, and Ike and I both remembered the story of Tamishan. We returned to complete our chores. It seemed that no matter what we did during the day, there was always something else that had to be done. Through the fall, Mr. Wilford or somebody would be shucking and shelling corn. Most of the corn would be used to fatten up the hogs, which would be killed before Thanksgiving. That was the way Mr. Wilford had done it last year and the years before that and would do it this year and the next year and the next and so on. It was a never ending cycle of jobs to be done. We shucked and shelled corn until noon. That day, Miss Lucille and Miss Esther prepared special lunches for us. After Mr. Wilford arrived, Miss Lucille called, "Lunch is ready, boys! Come in and wash your hands."

Now, they knew Mr. Wilford well enough to know that he was not going to go for anything special. So, if it was going to be special, he better not feel like it was special. He was like that. We washed in the newly installed bathroom at the end of the now enclosed back porch. Mr. Wilford's hands never looked totally clean. They were hard and worn. The calluses on his hands reflected all the hard work he had experienced over his lifetime. Even at my age, I could see that they had character. We walked into the kitchen where the Carsons always ate and sat down at the green and yellow enameled metal table. Miss Esther fixed our plates and Miss Lucille served them to us. They had fried chicken with rice and gravy, corn on the cob that already had the butter dripping from the sides of the corn, green beans with onions and tomatoes, fried okra, a beet salad, and a mound of freshly baked biscuits direct from the oven. Mr. Wilford sat down and bowed his head. We assumed that he said grace, but we never heard him say a word.

He said, "Cille, get me some black berry jelly."

"Here it is, Uncle Wilford," as Miss Lucille, his sister, called him.

Ike said, "Could I have some more of that sweet tea, please?"

Miss Esther poured the tea and both sisters watched us eat, getting as much pleasure from seeing us enjoy the meal as they could get from eating it themselves.

"We sure are going to miss you, Ike," Miss Lucille ventured.

"Don't worry, I'll be back," Ike replied. "I like Morganton."

After we had finished eating, Mr. Wilford said that he wanted to see us in the back yard for a moment. We followed him to the back porch and down the steps. We all walked over to the middle of the yard and stood under the cherry tree. We knew that he was going to pay us for our work. Mr. Wilford had made us leave the kitchen because he was about to conduct "men's business." It couldn't be done in the presence of women.

Mr. Wilford said, "You boys did a fine job helping me all summer and I want you to know that I appreciate it. Here's two dollars for each of you. Now you can take the rest of the day off because I know that you, Ike, have to get ready to leave tomorrow. Thank you boys again for all your help this summer and good luck in school."

I gathered up my courage and decided to tell Mr. Wilford that I could not work for him any more. I reluctantly began, "Mr. Wilford, you know that I won't able to help you this fall because I have to go to school. Miss Esther asked me if I could take care of her front yard, seeing that Rev. Carson is ill and she has so many visitors coming in to see him. I said I thought I could do that."

"That's between you and her," was his only reply.

On the way home, I told Ike that Miss Esther had said that she would give me a dollar a week to sweep off her front porch and steps in the mornings before I went to school. I asked Ike, "Do you realize that I will be getting from her in four weeks, what Mr. Wilford paid us for working for him all summer?"

We walked on over to Aunt Lillian's house. We went upstairs where Ike packed his clothes, getting ready to leave.

"I am going to miss you, Ike."

"I am going to miss you, too. But you see, you will just be missing me, but I will be missing Aunt Lillian, DePapa, Uncle Toots, Aunt Mary, Mr. Wilford—everybody."

We didn't say much after that. I lay on the bed and thought about how much I had grown up during this summer. I had overcome my fear of darkness and all that lurks in the night. I had worked like a man for Mr. Wilford. I had learned how to ride a horse bareback, kill a chicken, make cement, plant all types of crops, plow a field, and French kiss. I had not dropped one thing and broken it during the summer. Kids had stopped calling me "Runaway," even though some continued to call me "Flathead." The important thing was that I did not care. It did not bother me anymore. I was much stronger this summer than I had been last summer. I no longer felt sorry for myself. I knew that I could do anything I wanted to do and be good at it. And best of all, I had made a friend out of a cousin. While DePapa may have wanted Ike to learn from me, I had learned as much from Ike. Ike was already going into his manhood and he had shown me the way.

Just then, Uncle John and Uncle Louie drove up in Uncle John's black 1950 Plymouth. I thought, "Only Uncle John has a car older than Daddy's!" After they had greeted everybody, we all went into the dining room, where Aunt Lillian had dinner already on the table. After dinner, we moved to the front yard to sit under the wisteria to enjoy the cool breeze of late August. DePapa sat in his chair surrounded by his family. There was Aunt Lillian, Uncle John, Uncle Louie, Dad, Mother, Tommy, Jimmy, Patricia, and Ike and me. Edith Mae drove Uncle Noah over in her car and Edie walked over from Burkemont Avenue with Aunt Clare. Oliver and Izola, who had been classmates of Uncle John's at Shaw, came by to speak to John and Louie. Miss Frankie and Miss Hester came by to say hello and then went over to Rev. Carson's house and joined Lucille and Esther on their front porch.

Tommy Peterson waved as he walked by and Mr. Clark tilted his hat with his right hand on the rim. A white man drove up in his open bed truck and asked if we wanted what was surely to be the last of the summer watermelons and cantaloupes.

DePapa said, "Leave 'em all on the bank."

DePapa had developed a habit of buying melons and giving them away to anyone who wanted one. I could remember the first time I had seen him do this. A white man had driven up in a buckboard pulled by an old mule. DePapa bought all his melons, but only after he had plugged one and tasted it.

But DePapa did not have this man plug his melons. I guess it didn't matter whether they were good or bad. They were the last of the season.

Will came by, sat on the front steps and lit his pipe.

I could hear "In the Still of the Night" coming from a radio in the window.

I felt a sense of peace. The family had gathered as they had done for generations. Somehow I knew that however Ike and I turned out in this world, it would be because of the strength we got from our family.

EPILOGUE

The Carsons and most of the neighbors of my youth have passed away. So have my grandparents, aunts, and uncles. The only remaining uncle was John (my namesake), my father's last brother, who died early in 2005. DePapa died in 1960. Dad asked the male grandchildren to serve as pallbearers at the funeral. DePapa was buried in Olive Hill Cemetery in Morganton on a bright, cold winter day like his parents before him and his children after him. He was buried in the family plot on land donated to the African American community of Morganton by his wife, Rebecca Fleming. Land from the legacy she had received from her white ancestor, Hamp Avery. Aunt Lillian died in 1998 after a short illness. As I stood in the cemetery on that warm summer day in June and watched my Aunt Lillian being laid to rest, I thought about my youth and the days we played in our wonderland. I remembered the many summers Aunt Lillian, DePapa, Tommy, Patricia and I spent cleaning the family plot and burning off dead grass in Olive Hill Cemetery. I even remembered the time I became too enthusiastic with the fire and nearly set the entire cemetery ablaze. I chuckled to myself as I cried for my dear Aunt Lillian as she assumed her place among the ancestors.

When my brother Jimmy finished high school, he went to barber college in Raleigh and lived with my Uncle John and Aunt Hortense. When Jimmy finished his training, he went back to Morganton and worked for Elbert Crisp until Elbert retired. At that time, Jimmy bought the same barbershop that our grandfather William Hennessee had opened near the turn of the 20th century in Morganton. So the Crisp Barbershop has gone full circle from Hennessee to Crisp back to (Hennessee) Fleming; my father and mother couldn't be more proud of Jimmy and how well he has run the business. He is a well-respected member of the Morganton business community and he has made a good living for his wife Linda, my former classmate, and his three children, just as my mother said her father William Emory Hennessee made a good living for his family in the early part of the 20th century from the same barbershop.

My cousin Ike returned to Durham where he continued his education in the Durham city schools. Upon leaving school, Ike was employed by the Carolina Block Company. For over a quarter century, Ike worked for the same company, seldom missing a day at work. He was a member of Mount Gilead Baptist Church. In 1974, Ike married Ruth Shaw and had one son, Isaac Cornelius Fleming, Jr. Ike, unfortunately, suffered from Diabetes like his father Louis and his paternal grandmother Rebecca Fleming. Ike died June 24, 1984 at Duke University Hospital from complications of the disease. He was buried at Glenview Memorial Park in Durham, North Carolina.

I graduated from Olive Hill High School in 1962, moved away from Morganton, and never returned there to live again. However, I have often returned to visit my parents, family, and friends. I am anchored in the African American community in Morganton, and it continues to provide the bedrock on which I have built my life and work. I attended and graduated from Berea College in 1966 with a BA degree in history. After college, I joined the Peace Corps and spent two years in Malawi, Africa. I received both the MA and Ph.D. degrees from Howard University in Washington, D.C., where I majored in American history and minored in African history. I married my college sweetheart, Barbara, in 1970. My older daughter, Tuliza, was born in 1972 and my younger daughter, Diara, was born in 1977. Barbara, a Ph.D. trained psychologist, is an author in her own right. She has published two mystery novels from her Matthew Alexander mystery series.

During my career in the museum field, I spent approximately 20 years at the Ohio Historical Society developing, establishing and directing the National Afro-American Museum and Cultural Center in Wilberforce, Ohio. I also served as the Director and Chief Operating Officer of the National Underground Railroad Freedom Center in Cincinnati, Ohio, prior to assuming my current position as Vice President of Museums at the Cincinnati Museum Center.

Memories of growing up in Morganton are as vivid to me today as they were in 1956, and the values I learned growing up in the small African-American community of Morganton, North Carolina, have remained with me all of my life.